"*Traces of Time* is a book of insinuating wisdom and delight. The poems are lyric, lucid, and often brief, but they never feel slight because they ponder, on a tangibly human scale, the secrets of existence. . . . There are few books of poems in which I like every poem. This is one of them."
—Dana Gioia

"Translator Anthony Molino first introduced Mariani's poetry to the English world more than a decade ago, and now he brilliantly provides this ampler selection, spanning four decades, which broadens our view of Mariani and confirms his importance. Molino has single-handedly made Mariani matter in English."
—Geoffrey Brock

"I can think of no contemporary poetry I would rather be reading at this moment. . . . Lucio Mariani writes with immense tenderness and grace, with remarkable density and swiftness."
—Mark Rudman

"Mariani has emerged as one of the few significant post-Montalian poets in Italy, and Molino is a graceful, experienced, thoroughly reliable translator. The result is an elegant book, an important book, bringing a distinctive voice into English."
—Rosanna Warren

"It is dimension, remove, reflection, epiphany that Mariani wishes for us—and gives us if we can find it. Would that we all could."
—Van K. Brock, *Literary Imagination*

Also by Lucio Mariani
in English Translation

Echoes of Memory:
Selected Poems of Lucio Mariani

LUCIO MARIANI

TIME
TRACES OF

NEW AND SELECTED POEMS

Translated from the Italian by Anthony Molino
Preface by Rosanna Warren

OPEN LETTER
LITERARY TRANSLATIONS FROM THE UNIVERSITY OF ROCHESTER

Dante epigraph on page 87 is from the 1957 translation by John Ciardi.

Library of Congress Cataloging-in-Publication Data:

Mariani, Lucio, 1936-
    [Poems. Selections. English & Italian]
    races of time : new and selected poems / Lucio Mariani ; translated by
Anthony Molino ; preface by Rosanna Warren. — First Edition.
        pages cm.
    Bilingual text in English and Italian ; translated from the Italian.
    ISBN 978-1-940953-14-4 (paperback) — ISBN 1-940953-14-6 (paperback)
    1. Mariani, Lucio, 1936—Translations into English. I. Molino, Anthony,
1957- translator. II. Warren, Rosanna, writer of preface. III. Title.
    PQ4873.A6948A2 2015
    851'.914—dc23
                                            2014047885

This project is supported in part by an award from the National Endowment for the Arts.

ART WORKS.
arts.gov

Printed on acid-free paper in the United States of America.

Text set in Jenson Pro, an old-style serif typeface drawn by Robert Slimbach, based on a Venetian old-style text face cut by Nicolas Jenson in 1470.

Design by N. J. Furl

Open Letter is the University of Rochester's nonprofit, literary translation press:
Lattimore Hall 411, Box 270082, Rochester, NY 14627

www.openletterbooks.org

CONTENTS

In memory of Justin Vitiello
—A. M.

PREFACE

By Rosanna Warren

They seem written in a late style, the work of an old man coolly contemplating his own death, these poems of Lucio Mariani in *Traces of Time*. But this collection comprises poems that span nearly forty years, selected and translated by Anthony Molino from Mariani's larger *Farfalla e segno: Poesie 1972-2009*. And it becomes clear that Mariani has always had "a late style." Schooled in the poetry and myths of Ancient Greece and Rome as in the ironies of Cavafy and the grim Moderns, he has always been contemplating his own death and the acerbities of life. As he claimed in "Poets," an ode from his earlier *Echoes of Memory*, "Players of superfluousness / they know by heart / the rules of the void."

Responding to the void, Mariani has devised a range of tones, from severe understatement, to bitter personal address, to passionate, full-throated poems of celebration and mourning. Throughout, however, he reminds us of poetry's marginal status, and it is with a stoic sense of the absurd that he keeps making his songs. But make them he does, unrepentantly, and with the pride of belonging to an ancient fellowship he answers Auden's famous declaration that "poetry makes nothing happen": "You, however, dissent, and counter out loud / that art makes beauty happen" ("The Knaves of Commerce"). Mariani's forms of beauty are terse and stripped of illusions, except, perhaps, the last illusion of form itself as worthy of devotion.

And what illusions do his poems cast off? He might be mistaken, at times, for a nostalgic grouch and a crank, mourning for a lost Golden Age of classic dignity. Certainly, he keeps an inventory of contemporary decadence. In the modernity he observes, "No one comes anymore with word / of the oracles" ("Crèche"); the new vulgarians wrench the corpses of Renaissance nobles out of their graves, so that "It no longer suffices to protect one's life, / we now need also to preserve our death" ("Operation Medici"). But in the larger perspective of these poems, and they do lay out a much larger perspective, the oracles were always suspect and humans were always prey to dangerous illusions and greed. Mariani's classicism presents a dark school in human nature and its fate. In "New Myths," he personifies the contemporary violence of war in the ancient image of the Bull of Mithra, "The bull of destinies, thundering, reckless, soars / ravaging Asian skies . . ." If we neglect or scorn the classics today at our peril, it is not because they could have comforted us, but because they could have alerted us to our own worst selves, the barbarians within us ("What Barbarians").

It is in his poems of antiquity that Mariani finds his deepest voice, and that mixture of beauty, danger, decrepitude, and courage that gives amplitude to his vision:

> Three hours since daybreak, and still the sun struggles to pierce
> the pines of Aleppo, ecstatic guardians of silence.
> Ephesus is here, like a pink spore left on the slope
> by Etesian winds, ruffled in its random flight . . .
>
> ("Ephesus")

He finds that mixture also in his erotic poems. Some of these poems are almost cruelly disillusioned. Romance seems to have ebbed from scenes like this one in "Love Sometimes":

> Habit makes for a roll call of sorts
> the room opens and I begin as usual
> the games I really don't want to play
> the same games she's not keen on . . .

In "Desert," "And no one will someday discover / who between us delivered the final blow." Yet as in the abraded land of "Ephesus," where "fragments of thorn / and bone . . . still now scourge the mind with mysteries," love too still flares against the void for the aging poet. "Embrace me, embrace me," he cries in "Against All Daggers": "Let me fall / like a drop / slipping in the folds of your fan."

Against meaninglessness, against waste, against violence, against the gods who seem, in Mariani's imagination, more the wanton destroyers of Euripides than the justices of Aeschylus, humans make love and make poems, and Mariani's poems have the determination and gallantry to celebrate that secret joy. It is both secret and not secret, since the poem makes a gift of it to those who can decipher the signs. The whole poem, "The Envy of the Gods," declares that faith:

THE ENVY OF THE GODS

> Speak softly, feign and lie about these our days
> for the gods inhabit even the leaves of olive trees
> the unadorned petals of the pink camellia, the weave
> of feathers that robin redbreast flaunts at the world.

For they hearken in the lemon grove, hide
in the thick of the bush, in trickles of water
that spring, rare and sudden, like a news flash
from a face of stone, there, in the edge
of the pillow that frames your features. Remember,
their envy takes no step back
but schools us never to reveal our joy.

TRANSLATOR'S NOTE

"I was born in Rome and, as a result, I believe in the discipline of irony and in its fundamental, healing function. It's difficult to define the vast territory of a certain Roman spirit that still exists, and of all that Rome has to offer: its timeless beauty, a beauty forever mixed with wonder and surprise; its abundance, and the constant and revolutionary display of the baroque; a certain openness, evidenced in the readiness of Romans to smile and greet most anyone; its irony and *supercilium*—a way of knitting the eyebrows to show severity and silent anger; the fruitfulness of amazement and the seduction of the unspoken; its indifference to the ravages of time; its obsession with an inexhaustible debt toward the world, and the habit of keeping what is most cherished locked in one's heart."

—Lucio Mariani

✦

A little over a decade ago, I had the good fortune of introducing into English one of Italy's finer contemporary poets, Lucio Mariani. In my note to his selected poems, *Echoes of Memory* (Wesleyan UP, 2003),

I had this to say: "Within a lyrically saturated culture such as ours, infused with the kind of celebration of the ego that characterizes so much confessional poetry, Mariani's verse points to both difference and need. His work restores to the lyric—through images both dense and porous, lines both cadenced and spasmodic—an ancestral, mythical sensibility that reminds us of our place in history today, at the start of a dizzying and displacing millennium. It is a poetry that reclaims for itself a centering and ethical function—which is different, say, from a denouncing or moralizing one. Along these lines, in reading Mariani, one is reminded of the quality embodied by Eugenio Montale, or William Meredith: poets whose elevated but subdued tones, in celebrating the pietas and pathos of our condition, everywhere betray a defining commitment to a timeless human capacity for both integrity and doubt."

This assessment remains timely in now choosing to render into English an ample selection from Mariani's *Farfalla e segno: Poesie 1972-2009* (Milan, Crocetti Editore, 2010), which revisits and updates the poet's production of nearly forty years. It is an assessment that is moreover enhanced by Gallimard's 2005 publication of *Connaissance du temps*, a translation of Mariani's *Qualche notizia del tempo* (Crocetti, 2001) by the renowned Michel Orcel that situates Mariani—by way of Gallimard's series "Domaine Italien"—in the company of celebrated Italian writers ranging from Verga to Magris. Moreover, as Charles Dobzynski convincingly argues in the feature article of the December 2005 issue of the distinguished French literary journal *Aujourd'hui Poème*, there is a timeliness to Mariani that links him to Pasolini, Luzi, and Raboni, poets who managed to transcend the immediacy of their historical contexts by grappling with the demons of history. To this end, Dobzynski quotes the postscript to the Gallimard edition by Jean-Baptiste Para (who in turn evokes Brodsky): *"Le poète n'est pas seulement contemporain de son époque, il est contemporain de la nuit des temps."* ("The poet is not only a contemporary of his age, but of the night of all ages.")

Indeed, much of Mariani's recent work exemplifies the relationship between poetry and history. A relationship that cannot be contextualized within the limits of any *koiné*, but tends nonetheless to size up those events that affect the global space of the one and only polis in which we all live. To measure itself against the history of its own time is a constant of poetry, a part of the very dynamics of the art. Certainly, not all poetry is so deliberately and consciously embattled—and nor is most of Mariani's. But the very fact that poetry lives and nourishes itself outside of organized systems, that it blossoms *à l'écart* in the merry-go-round of days, that it endures in the millenary game of the soul's forging, makes of it without a doubt a form of counterpower: a glance that situates itself in opposition to the storylines of history. And it is in casting such glances that Mariani goes unequalled. Several poems in this collection illustrate and support this claim—"Tiananmen Square, 20 Years Later," or "Protocols of War," to mention just two—but none perhaps more successfully than the solemn verses of "Checkmate."

Concerning this poem, which closed out my first book of Mariani's (the poem was unpublished in Italian at the time, and is here retained) I can do no better than to quote from Robert Zaller's review of *Echoes of Memory* (*Rain Taxi* 9-1, spring 2004):

> The collection concludes, startlingly, with an evocation of the September 11 disaster . . . "Checkmate" is not only a compassionate elegy for a particular loss, but a reminder of the vulnerability of the city and hence of civilization itself in the post-Hiroshima age. Now that all history and memory can be annihilated in the blink of an eye, the poet's task has become problematic in a way

that Dante, for example . . . could never have imagined. Mariani's response is to persevere in the disembodied consciousness of his hero, beseeching the woman he had been destined to meet to "ask the white irises / to bloom in my name, faded, erased." Thus, while Mariani says elsewhere that the poet has only "alphabets of surrender" and the "rhyme of clear silence," the impulse remains "to cry the poem that is ours alone."

As Mariani puts it: "What I wanted to do was to let the young victim speak, express his surprise and pain in the face of the event: a pain silenced, of course, by the event itself, which loses its centrality because the only important focus is on the young man who will die under the atrocity of the bomb, with nothing left to teach or pass on to anyone. What is heard through the voice of this young man is the condemnation of absurdity. It is his disappearance that speaks, and not the event." What speaks, in other words, is a fateful trace of time . . .

But let me add another example. A second poem from *Traces of Time*, "New Myths," was written in 2002, when the Palestinian question—today, again, tragically "current"—exploded in a vicious cycle of violence that the Western world essentially ignored. Claiming that history is moved less by the actions of heroes than by the errors of the indifferent, the poet takes on this guilty neglect and makes it his own. The poem opens with a metaphorical image (the bull of destinies) taken from the Veda and the cult of Mithras: this wild bull, the first creature of the God Ahura-Mazda, must be killed in order for life and goodness to gush forth from his blood. (The image, of course, also derives from the Greek myth of the rape of Europa.) Fundamentally, this metaphor of devastation is a mirror in

xvi

which reality confronts a gross and otherwise inconceivable image of itself, of what it has become. The mirror must be smashed, the bull destroyed, and reality transformed. Not unlike the task of any true poet who, like Mariani, opposes the tyranny of the present through the focused and relentless discipline of his craft.

◆

"Reading Mariani beside many American peers can seem a study in contrasting contemporaneity . . . Does poetry need to do more than be present, observing the present given? There have been strong forces in American poetry for the last half century that directly counter the more traditional western poetic that Mariani asserts . . . It is dimension, remove, reflection, epiphany that Mariani wishes for us—and gives us if we can find it. Would that we all could."

So concludes a review of *Echoes of Memory* by Van K. Brock (*Literary Imagination*, vol.7, no. 3, fall 2005). Brock here spells out the amplitude of Mariani's engagement with time. Dimension, remove, reflection, and epiphany: stances and sensibilities nourished, as Brock wryly states, over "an allusive range of a few thousand years." "I imagine Mariani in Rome," he continues, "where the buildings speak and the ruins every few hundred yards accuse us of forgetfulness . . ." It is precisely the laxity of memory, the weakened sense of the pulse of our bloodlines, and the dominant culture's perverse visual wizardry and adulation of the ephemeral that compels Mariani's stoic testimony, and fuels the power of his imagery. Few writers **today** can so *naturally* **and** *convincingly* summon up images of a "seaman's surprise"

("The Gesture"), or of a fountain's "face of stone" ("The Envy of the Gods"); of a moody and mercurial "kingdom of law" (*L'esprit de la loi*), whose capriciousness, especially in recent Italian history, has made for resounding windfalls and downfalls. Few can so movingly pay homage to a translator ("To a Translator") or depict and ennoble the reality of old age ("Talking to Themselves"). And few, moreover, are so *present to* and *engaged by* their time as to create in Italian some of the finest *poesia civile* since Pasolini: I'm thinking here of poems like Mariani's "What Barbarians"—where he denounces the pernicious and self-righteous racism of so many of his countrymen, threatened by throngs of destitute immigrants in turn rejected as "barbarian" invaders; or like "Oration," where the Madrid terrorist bombing of 2004 makes for a resounding and lucid appeal for the cultivation and *resistance* of our species' saner instincts and sentiments. (Both these poems, more than ten years later, read as if they were written today: when Lampedusa is overrun daily by hundreds of desperate and oft-smuggled Africans, and ISIS terrorizes the Middle East, and the West, with its decapitations and genocides.)

But perhaps one of America's own finer poets, Mark Rudman, said it best when introducing Mariani to a New York audience, soon after *Echoes of Memory* was published: "I can think of no contemporary poetry I would rather be reading at this moment; there is no defeat here, no caving in to oppressive pressures of which the war in Iraq, for instance, is clearly just a symptom. *Echoes of Memory* is about the war in our hearts, from which imagination may fashion a few redeeming images; images, he reminds us, not thoughts. Lucio Mariani writes with immense tenderness and grace, with remarkable density and swiftness. His work enacts an intriguing dialogue with the poetry of the past, the problem of writing poetry at all. It has both the quality of presence and selflessness. It is an appealing accomplishment to evoke a romantic tone, like an echo of memory, with and for the sparest accompaniment." Like an echo of memory or, again, like a trace of time.

✦

In closing, a few words about the translation. I have a distinctly personal metaphor for my translation work. I like to think of myself as a "gentleman thief," someone à la Cary Grant transposed to the world of letters. Better yet, someone who has slipped into the home of a single poet, often through the window of a single book of a very special artist I've studied and long spied on. When a translation of mine "works," when it satisfies me to the point that I want to see it published, "domesticated" in the pages of another book, something strange happens: I can tend to forget there was an original poem, that the appropriated object first "belonged" to someone else. Indeed, I can forget there were any objects stolen. Like for thieves who steal for the pleasure of possession, a delusion sets in whereby the original poetic object becomes mine, and the process of appropriation (translation) ends up erasing any memory of the theft. It's as if the poem were always mine, penned by me in English from the get-go. Admittedly, perhaps pathologically narcissistic if not sociopathic, this attitude—if it is to function—must however end up honoring the poet and the original poem. Always. For if it doesn't, the translation is lacking, and has failed. Leaving traces of nothing more than a botched theft. My hope, then, in once again presenting a few dozen gems from the collection of Mr. Mariani, is that no suspicion will be raised, for a fleeting but hopefully imperishable moment, as per their provenance.

I would like to acknowledge those who helped bring this project to fruition. Marina Molino, Paul Feinberg, Sarah Spence, and Aaron Kerner all graciously supported the project at different stages of its conception. The noteworthy journals *Two Lines* and *Literary Imagination* both hosted earlier versions of some of the translations here included; the essay that closes out *Traces of Time* was also published in *Literary Imagination* (vol.7, n.1, 2005). Suzanna Tamminen at Wesleyan University Press has very graciously given permission to reprint several poems from Mariani's *Echoes of Memory*, thus honoring the poet's longstanding inclination to carry over from previous collections a number of poems into his newest book. Ergo, as has been Mariani's wont in Italian, so we manage in English! Rosanna Warren has been the staunchest and truest of advocates in her unflagging commitment to Mariani's and my work—and for this my gratitude endures. Jennifer Grotz goes recognized for her editorial acumen and courage in recommending *Traces of Time* for publication to Open Letter Books, where Kaija Straumanis has been an invaluable, reliable, and ever-present resource. Finally, alongside my heartfelt thanks to Lucio Mariani and his wife, Carlotta, for their generous and dignified friendship of twenty years, I would like to dedicate this book to Anna Zambon, whose bountiful Tuscan hospitality over many summers afforded me the time and solace to complete the translation.

Anthony Molino

TRACES OF TIME

AGONE

Domandavi se mai mi sentissi in ritardo.
È un problema di chi si mette fra la seconda
e l'ultima corsia.
Io rincorro da solo.
Che sia quindi in anticipo o tardivo
tutto dipende dal disamore che sto ruminando.
Per la giusta cadenza ho battuto le mani due o tre volte
e mi sono premiato schizzandomi sul viso
fresche parcelle di felicità. Nel buio.

CONTEST

You'd ask if I were ever late.
That's a problem for people stuck
between the second and last lanes.
Me, I'm in lone pursuit.
So that whether I'm early or late
depends solely on the day's disaffection.
To catch the beat I clapped my hands once or twice,
before splashing my face with particles
of happiness. For getting it right. In the dark.

MI DIRAI

Come amore soltanto ti vivo assente
amore mio
deposta nella trama
e nella corda un filo indistinguibile,
continuato fremòre del silenzio.
Mi dirai non è amore, così non è
dolore il non patito, il temuto dolore
tu che non sai cominciata la morte
e che cerchi le affiches sopra ogni bottiglia.

YOU'LL SAY

I live your love only in your absence
my love
stitched in the woof
and weft of an invisible thread
endless throb of silence.
That's not love, you'll say, the way pain
not suffered, though dreaded,
isn't pain. You, who ignore that death has set in
and trust the label on every bottle.

DOVE

Dove il rumore della tua memoria
stagna forte, sottile, inconsumato
ubique lune e stelle differenti
dicono quanto passo della notte
di quante notti ancora sto passando
per trovare rarissime finzioni
da versare sul petto e sull'attesa
della piccola morte che m'hai dato.

WHERE

Where the din of your memory
stagnates strong subtle unconsumed
everywhere moons and disparate stars
tell how much of the night I pass
how many nights I still pass looking
to find the rarest of pretences
to pour over my chest and the wait
for the little death you handed me.

L'AMORE TALVOLTA

Chiama l'usanza un minimo di appello,
s'apre la stanza e avvio secondo norma
i giochi che non voglio interamente
che come me non vuole interamente
la conosciuta mia.
E pure si converge e pure si conviene
per un curioso, banale istinto di compattamento.
Eppure avviene.

LOVE SOMETIMES

Habit makes for a roll call of sorts
the room opens and I begin as usual
the games I really don't want to play
the same games she's not keen on.
And still we meet, still we converge
by way of some odd, banal inclination to conjoin.
The pact, you know,
just happens.

L'ALTRO

Mi chiedi d'esser l'altro che comprendi,
quello che parla lentamente, chiaro,
che descrive le piazze partendo dai negozi
che del mare
discute il salino, il rischio, la grandezza
che lasci la sera
ritrovi il mattino inalterato.
Mi chiedi d'esser l'altro
che cadenza la cura
dell'orto e del tuo frutto
acqua per l'acqua
fronte per la fronte
che morde con i denti
e il giorno divide dalla notte,
non cerca indizi di luna.
Mi chiedi d'esser l'altro
che conosce per nome
i suoi nemici e il giusto
che non lima un dubbio rotondo
che sputa le spine del ventre
che lo scriccio di foglia calpestata
chiama rumore.

Mi chiedi d'esser biondo.

THE OTHER

You ask me to be the other you comprehend,
the one who speaks slowly, clearly,
who describes a piazza from its shops
and discusses the sea's
salinity, its risk and grandeur
whom at night you leave
to find in the morning, unchanged.
You ask me to be the other
who cadences the care
of your garden and fruit
water for water
brow for brow
who bites with his teeth
to divide night from day,
indifferent to the moods of the moon.
You ask me to be the other
who knows what's right
and his enemies by name,
who smooths the edges of doubt
and spits up the thorns in his gut,
who calls the crackle of a leaf underfoot
noise.

You ask me to be blond.

L'ETERNITÀ

a Luca

Mentre l'eternità figlio,
l'eternità è quel modo di te
che ho potuto donarti stabilmente,
un tralcio sotterrato
nel parco dei tuoi umori
che riaffiora nel sorriso improvviso
nell'inabilità della mano a sfabbricare
nella curiosità che ti dà il mare
forte e continua più della paura
nel rispettare il misero antropino
nell'amore del vino e delle poppe.
Eterna figlio è la tua parte
eterno quel milligrammo mio
che domani ed insieme ingombreranno
il gesto della scimmia tua devota
qualunque sia
per sangue o suggestione. E così via.

ETERNITY

for Luca

Whereas eternity, my son,
eternity is that way of yours
I managed indelibly to bestow,
a brier hidden
in the garden of your moods
that sprouts in your sudden smile
in your hand's inability to craft
in the curiosity the sea inspires
stronger and steadier than any fear
in your respect for the lowly little man
in your love for wine and tits.
Eternal, my son, is the part of you
eternal that milligram of mine
that tomorrow together will burden
the gesture
of any and every monkey devoted to you
whether by blood or influence. And so on.

Y ENTONCES

a César Vallejo

Salve infinito Vallejo
sproposito umano
salve cuore capace del tuo corpo
dei mille amati e d'oltre
salve voce che hai detto
quello che il tempo ancora tace
salve unico mastro nell'impresa
di restare tradito post mortem
salve luce della candela malintesa
liquidato con quattro righe
nel dictionnaire di Van Tieghem
contro le ventitré per Alberti il corista
salve spada emotiva della guerra
combattuta da solo
sudando inchiostro d'anima e di sale.
Sulle ciglia
raccolgo i resti della devozione
e t'accarezzo
felice che di te abbiano fatto
un mio segreto
César Vallejo, miniera generale
di quozienti estricabili nonché
di chiavi di cappelli y entonces.

1974

Y ENTONCES

for César Vallejo

Hail, infinite Vallejo
human blunder
hail, heart worthy of your body
of the thousands loved and more
hail, voice that spoke
what time still hushes
hail, lone master adept
at staying betrayed post-mortem
hail, light of a misguided candle
dismissed in but four lines
by Van Tieghem in his *dictionnaire*
while Alberti the chorister counts twenty-three
hail, emotive sword of the war
you fought alone
sweating ink of soul and salt.
From my eyes I wipe
the remains of my devotion
and I embrace you
happy they have made of you
my own personal secret.
César Vallejo, universal mine
of all that can be extracted from words,
of keys of hats *y entonces*.

1974

LETTERA

a Carlotta

Non è facile, amata
portare a spalla il cerchio dell'assenza
tra le marche gualcite di tabacco
e dischi crocefissi.
E non è buono
masticare l'aspro vuoto
che offende stanze più magre
copre l'annuncio magico dei fiori
m'invade occhi e ragione come un grido.
Non è facile, amata
diradare le foglie del silenzio
e travedere il caracollo del mio stambecco
quando chiude la corsa sorridente
ritornato alla valle longobarda
fra bricconieri che attendono alla posta
dietro il grasso songino.
Lo so, lo so che al mare nasce più raro
il cespo ed impervìo, difficile a strappare
lo so, lo so che in branco la paura si svende
e il tiglio del consenso accarezza i tuoi sogni
lo so, lo so che i figli chiedono pane
e più chiedono carne.
Non è facile, amata
farti capire con le mani e gli occhi
che qui si può svernare per la vita
dove t'amiamo in due, il luccio ancora bravo

LETTER

for Carlotta

It's not easy, my love
to shoulder the circle of absence
amid crumpled cigar labels
and crucified LPs.
And it's not good
to chew on the acrid emptiness
that offends emaciated rooms
covers the magic flowers announce
invades my eyes and mind like a scream.
It's not easy, my love
to thumb through the leaves of silence
and glimpse the gambol of my wild goat,
its run over, smiling, home again
in its Longobard valley among poachers
in ambush behind the plump blackberry.
I know, I know that bushes are rarely
born by the sea, and hard to uproot
I know, I know that fear comes cheap among the horde
and that fruits of harmony caress your dreams
I know, I know that the children ask for bread
and more, they ask for flesh.
It's not easy, my love
for my hands and eyes to make you understand
that here we can spend the winter for life
where two of us will love you,
the spry jackfish

e il tuo poeta nei quaranta brandelli
in due definiti come i giri del tronco.
Non è facile, amata
rivelarti perché nessun delitto
ha fatto un morto solo.

and your poet in tatters
both, definitive, like the rings of a tree trunk.
It's not easy, my love
to reveal you, for no murder ever
claimed only one victim.

PROVA

D'inverno se pensi a una barca
e non sei marinaio
la vedi passare irta di bianche velerie
ai piedi d'un cielo stupefatto
sola e distante come una sposa disabitata
che il muto gabbiano accompagna
attraverso gli spazi d'un fondale di scena.
Dove l'onda non frange
né acqua così turchina potrà mai bagnarti.

Niente ritorna
e ogni barca che passa è perduta.

Tu non sei marinaio
prova a Natale
se mento.

TRY

In winter, if you think of a boat
and aren't a sailor
you see a bristling white canvass adrift
at the foot of a dumbfounded sky
alone faraway like a deserted bride
whom the mute seagull accompanies
across the backdrop of a stage
through spaces where no wave ever breaks
and never will turquoise waters spray you.

Nothing returns
and every boat that passes is lost.

You're no sailor
try proving me wrong
at Christmas.

GLI UNICI MORTI

"Une étincelle y pense à mes absents."
—P. Valéry, Le Cimetière marin

Fin quando ogni mia notte sarà invasa
dalle sagome amate di quei lari
che tornano in manipoli e sorrisi
a prendermi teneramente il viso
e a parlarmi con impeto
per cambiare disegno ai miei pensieri
come petali sparsi,
fino a quando il bel sogno durerà,
gli unici morti per me resteranno
soltanto i vivi che un qualunque giorno
di sole o pioggia
si chiusero alle spalle questa porta
senza mai più passare una notizia
e adesso se ne stanno su una sedia
inebetiti dal televisore
ad aspettare i numeri del lotto
a scordarsi dei figli in sala giochi, a comandare
eserciti e opifici, ad alzare di noia la sottana
o a servire un padrone di famiglia
a dare fondo fisso a una bottiglia
o a voltare pinnacoli e gabbana .
Naturalmente, nel novero si devono contare
quelli che hanno giostrato attorno al niente
e anche gli altri che assai discretamente

THE ONLY DEAD

"Une étincelle y pense à mes absents."
—P. Valéry, Le Cimetière marin

As long as my every night is invaded
by the beloved profiles of friends
who return in clusters, smiling
to cusp my face in their hands
and speak to me impassioned
about changing the forms of my thought
like scattered petals;
as long as the lovely dream endures
for me the only dead remain
the living who, on any given day
rain or shine
close this door behind them
never again for news to filter
and now lounge in a stupor
before the TV, waiting
for today's winning lottery numbers
forgetful of kids at their playstations, busy
running armies and opium dens, chasing skirts
out of boredom or playing yes-men
to godfathers, while gazing into the bottom of a bottle,
jumping ship or bandwagon.
Of course these likes will also count
those who flirted with the void
and others who, with utmost discretion,

sono andati a svanire silenziosi
nei plausibili flutti della prassi,
oltre l'ultima nebbia
dove affonda la corsia d'emergenza.

went on to disappear in silence
in the undertow of plausible routines
beyond the final haze where
the emergency lane founders.

COINCIDENZE

A te penso
uomo di Tenerife
qualsiasi mulatto sui cinquanta
che stai girando l'angolo e dietro al chiosco
pisci di buon umore sul muro polveroso
mentre ritorni a casa, alla casa di latta
avvolta nel benevolo dicembre.
Uomo di Tenerife
ti sto guardando
io che non esisto per te
dentro nessuna stanza della terra
né posso somigliare ad un profilo
della nuvola vaga
a te penso comunque
fratello immaginario e al fatto
che mai più sentirò la tua corsa
oltre il baleno
di questa evocazione solitaria
in una fredda notte d'Europa.
Penso a te nato forse nel mio giorno
che senza pena senza meraviglia
nello stesso mio giorno
morirai.

COINCIDENCES

I'm thinking of you
man from Tenerife
of any half-breed in his fifties
as you turn the corner and behind the kiosk
piss heartily against the crumbled wall
as you go home, to your four walls of tin
wrapped in this benevolent December.
Man from Tenerife
I look at you
I who don't exist for you
in any room on earth
nor can I resemble the outline
of a vague cloud
and yet I think of you
imaginary brother, and of the fact
that never again will I sense your course
beyond the flicker
of this solitary evocation
on a cold night in Europe
I think of you, born perhaps on my same day
stranger to pain and wonder
you who on my same day
will die.

SUL PRATO

Un manto di foglie lussuose m'accalora.
La tua lingua autunnale si spande
sulla pelle in pieghe di velluto, tenera
da irrorare i sogni. Come mi batte il cuoricino
nella vena di malva che gonfia la radice
e la sottende verso pergole in fiore.

IN THE GRASS

A bed of luscious leaves inflames me.
Your autumn tongue expands
across my skin in velvet folds, tenderly
irrigating my dreams. My wee heart
beats like mad, in the mauve vein that swells
the root and stretches for the sprouting trellis.

SULLA LINGUA

Femmine e spezie, a spalmarle sulla lingua,
tieni conto dei differenti porti di partenza
con quale inclinazione le colpirono raggi di sole
e bali della luna, quante arti le han confuse
e quante mani per renderle migliori ad incontrarti,
in che modo l'uso o l'abuso loro ti saprà conservare
nel sorriso.

ON THE TONGUE

Women and spices may linger on the tongue
but be mindful of their ports of origin
of the angle at which they're struck by the sun
and moonlight, of the arts that have confused them
and the many hands that favored your encounter,
of how the ways you use or misuse them
will figure into your smile.

GIOCHI D'ACQUA

Né una stella né un demone o un'avèrla
mi chiesero di esistere. Pure ti parla
ancora e ti sorride uno dei mille
e mille giochi d'acqua, un caso della forma,
la drupa lavorata dalle prove del tempo
fatta colma di sangue, che guardi ed accarezzi.

Né una stella né un demone domanderà
quando vorrò morire. Ma insiste l'ora e l'ombra
si propaga sulla spalla, insiste nelle frazioni
e i multipli a devastare puntigliosamente
mentre rifiuto il fratello sconosciuto
che mi rende
i suoi occhi malati dallo specchio.

Non mi chiede una stella di scrivere la vita
e con le dita stringere il sogno e la memoria.
Ma
la penna è l'ago della mia ferita.

WHIMS OF WATER

Neither a star nor a demon or shrike
asked me to exist. And yet this whim
of water speaks to you and smiles still, one
of countless thousands, a chance of form,
a crag cut by the course of time,
blood-soaked, that you probe and caress.

Neither a star nor demon will ask
when I'll want to die. But the hour presses,
its shadow looming over my shoulder,
with devastating precision its fractions
and multiples press as well while I
dismiss the unknown of kin
whose ill gaze eyes me from the mirror.

There's no star asking me to write my life,
to clasp with my fingers at the dream and memory.
But
this pen is what balances my wound.

EFESO

I

A tre ore dall'alba, ancora stenta il sole a farsi varco
tra i pini di Aleppo, estatici guardiani del silenzio.
Efeso è qui come una spora rosa lasciata sul pendio
da venti etèsi, scompaginata nello sciatto volo.
Efeso è qui vedova delle spume, un'esule di mare nelle spire
limose del piccolo Meandro, qui confitta e arenata
méndica il ventre antico di sponda estrema che accolse
Egeo nel disperato salto. Efeso è qui, memore di tramonti
convertiti nel bagliore di aurore occidentali,
quando dal porto le donne ionie vedevano salpare
intemerati i remieri di Focea e spargevano in acqua
le corone intrecciate con le foglie di vite e i gelsomini.

II

Per questa terra abrasa i nostri occhi di cane
rovistano i gomitoli del tempo, tutte le età rapprese
nelle vene delle colonne morse, lungo il petalo bruno
d'una cavèa sonora, tra i nomi consumati sulla pallida
stele abbandonata all'abbraccio di oliastri. Battiamo
i piedi dove rovescia il furore dei Cimmeri, dove
la Grande Madre versa seme di toro e lacrime dell'ape,
dove sgorga il discorso di Eraclito, un rivolo di fuoco
e di lapilli che scavalca i millenni e con le spine

EPHESUS

I

Three hours since daybreak, and still the sun struggles to pierce
the pines of Aleppo, ecstatic guardians of silence.
Ephesus is here, like a pink spore left on the slope
by Etesian winds, ruffled in its random flight.
Ephesus is here, widow of foaming seas, exile of waves mired
in the spirals of the lesser Maeander, here, riveted, shipwrecked
imploring the far-off ancient shore that embosomed Aegeus
in his desperate leap. Ephesus is here, mindful of sunsets
recast in the dazzling glow of western dawns,
when Ionian women watched from the harbor
as the intrepid oarsmen of Phocaea set sail, and decked the water
with wreaths braided from jasmine and grape leaves.

II

Across this abraded land these dog eyes of ours
scour the strands of time, the ages curdling
in the veins of gnawed columns, the sallow petal
of a clanging cavea, the names consumed on an ashen
stele abandoned to the embrace of oleasters. Our feet
tread there where the fury of the Cymry pounds, where
the Great Mother spills the seed of bulls and tears of bees,
where the word of Heraclitus gushes, stream of fire
and lapilli hurdling the millennia, fragments of thorn

e gli ossi del frammento ancora frusta di misteri la mente,
battiamo i piedi dove ripara Antonio a regalare
l'ultimo sorriso ai satiri e alle menadi.

III

Né il crocidio del corvo infrange il cielo né un pendolo
suadente di cicale. La via che sale e la via che scende
sono una sola e la stessa. Come fiori di marmo
dalle mille stagioni ininterrotte, ali di testimoni
corteggiano la strada dei Cureti e il passo che la solca,
vita e morte confuse nella formula immobile del tempo. Allora
queste nostre ombre sottili sono anche l'ombra di coloro
che spesero il destino per i secoli d'Efeso la Grande e nella luce
ora sorgono e sono. Al fondo del cammino, alte le fiamme
della devozione, brucia per sempre la biblioteca di Celso
e nel rogo lo scheletro solenne della pietra apre un mirario
che racconta agli dèi la storia d'una dedica filiale,
avventura interdetta agli immortali, onore degli umani.

and bone that still now scourge the mind with mysteries.
Our feet tread there where Antony takes refuge
to offer one final smile to the satyrs and maenads.

III

Neither the cawing crow nor a swaying pendulum
of cicadas shatters the sky. The way up and the way down
are one and the same. Like marble flowers
of a thousand uninterrupted seasons, wings of witnesses
court the road of the Curetes and our own fresh tracks,
life and death confused in the quiescent formula of time. Thus,
these wiry shadows of ours are also the shades of those
who spent their destiny for the centuries of Ephesus the Great,
who in the light now rise, and are. At the end of the road, amid
towering flames of devotion, burns forever the library of Celsus
wherein the solemn skeleton of stone opens a spiracle
to tell the gods a story of filial homage,
an adventure denied the immortals, a solely human honor.

PRESEPE

Nessuno oltre i cespugli dello stupore,
oltre la forma ironica del guscio.
E più nessuno arriva a portare notizie
degli oracoli. Sulla riva muschiata degli stagni
lungo i viali di ghiaia
dai monti dolci come seni innevati
tutto il presepe marcia sul posto,
le valige vuote, senz'ombra, senza sguardo,
sotto la trama delle stelle appese al soffitto di carta.
Né sorride per noi bianca la luna.

CRÈCHE

No one beyond the hedges of wonder,
beyond the ironic form of the shell.
No one comes anymore with word
of the oracles. On the mossy banks of ponds
along pebbly roads
down mountains soft as snow-capped breasts
the entire crèche marches in place
casting no shadows, bundles and gazes empty,
beneath the plot of stars dangling from a cardboard ceiling.
Nor does the white moon smile upon us.

BASTA IL PIÚ TENUE VENTO

Le donne muoiono d'autunno nel minimo clamore
quando qualunque amore è consumato. Ne sono garanti
le date incise in tutti i camposanti di monte e di mare.
Appena si fanno deserte di voci le stanze
le donne sono certe che altra attesa
non serve a intercettare l'avvenire
e alle prime luci d'autunno si staccano dal cuore
come foglie di gelso. Cadono docili sul fondo
nell'isolato annuncio di giornale, le presidiano
sillabe discrete di compianto.
Basta il piú tenue vento.

THE SLIGHTEST OF WINDS

Women die in autumn, in a hush,
when any love is long consumed. Just check the dates
chiseled in mountain and seaside graveyards.
No sooner do voices desert the rooms
than women know no further waiting is needed
to intercept the future,
and like mulberry leaves
they loosen from their hearts. And they flutter
to the bottom of a far-off obituary, guarded
by discreet syllables of grief.
The slightest of winds is enough.

IPERBOLE

La tua carne è materia
così seria
da palpare
con debita ironia
la sola salvifica distanza
che mi guardi
dalle ustioni
di falsa prospettiva.

HYPERBOLE

Your flesh
is such a serious matter
to be felt out
with due irony
the only saving distance
keeping me
from getting burned
by errors in perspective.

È NECESSARIO

L'attimo in cui finisce questo verso
nel verecondo battito di ciglia
al mondo nasce e brilla tanto male
da sventrare la vita.
Corrono
così gravi occasioni di pugnale
che per farti pittore
buon musico
elegante poeta
insomma per praticare con fervore l'arte
da trovare la meta dei suoi transiti
i soffi labili, le recondite carte
a palpebre serrate

                pellegrina la mente
è necessario
essere assente fino alla demenza
è necessario
riuscire a fare senza di chiunque
è necessario
restare sordo e fermo ad ogni grido
assediato da te
soltanto fido nel lento, ermo calvario
d'una stanza turrita
al riparo animale dal canto
dell'istanza morale
che da vie, mari e campi ti urla al cielo
quanto sa fare il male

IT'S NECESSARY

The instant this verse ends
in the veritable blink of an eye
so much evil will enter and dazzle the world
to leave life gutted.
So many are the menacing daggers
that to become a painter
a fine musician
or distinguished poet
to practice, that is, any art with passion
to fathom its destinations
and discern its murmurs, its storied papers
to focus fiercely
                        and free one's pilgrim mind
it's necessary
to take leave of that mind
necessary
to need no one
necessary
to remain steadfast, deaf to every cry
besieged by yourself alone
trusting in the slow and solitary agony
of an ironclad room
an animal safe from the song
of any moral outrage
that rants
to the skies from every sea, street and field
denouncing evil's sway

e dalla serratura ne bisbiglia le imprese
la cosmica bravura
l'opere estese
e nel sangue
l'ebrietudine permanente e azzurra.

whispering from the keyhole its feats
its cosmic wile
its far-reaching deeds
and in the blood its blue and everlasting
rapture.

L'INVIDIA DEGLI DÈI

Parla piano, dissimula e menti sui nostri giorni
gli dèi sono presenti anche tra le foglie dell'ulivo
tra i disadorni petali della camelia rosa, nella maglia
di piume che il pettirosso in posa ostenta al mondo.
Sono all'ascolto nella limonaia, al riparo
nel folto della macchia, dentro il filo d'acqua
che sgorga raro e improvviso come una notizia
dalla faccia di pietra, sono lì lungo il bordo
del cuscino che ti incornicia il viso. Ricorda sempre
che la loro invidia non arretra di un passo
e ti ammaestra a non scoprire mai la nostra gioia.

THE ENVY OF THE GODS

Speak softly, feign and lie about these our days
for the gods inhabit even the leaves of olive trees
the unadorned petals of the pink camellia, the weave
of feathers that robin redbreast flaunts at the world.
For they hearken in the lemon grove, hide
in the thick of the bush, in trickles of water
that spring, rare and sudden, like a news flash
from a face of stone, there, in the edge
of the pillow that frames your features. Remember,
their envy takes no step back
but schools us never to reveal our joy.

DE MORAES

Fu bello ascoltare Vinicius De Moraes
dire fra nota e nota che
la vita viene ad onde
come il mare.
Fu bello.
Ma Vinicius
mi tacque una costosa verità.
Che al termine, quanto resta dell'onda
ristagna in una pozza dove
sfiniti e radi arrivano altri spruzzi
e fa ombra il cespuglio di lacrime.

DE MORAES

It was swell listening to Vinicius De Moraes
say between one note and the next
that like the sea
life comes in waves.
It was swell.
But Vinicius
kept from me a costly truth.
That in the end, what's left of a wave
stagnates in a puddle where
later listless sprays peter out
and a shrub of tears casts its shadow.

LETE

Giorno o notte, all'ora indefinita
quando viene alla vita un verso grande,
una poesia vera, fosse per caso
fosse invenzione d'un nemico in arte

devi comprare una cravatta rossa
e vestirti di lino come si faceva
nella festa di Dio. Dopo leverai dalla testa
il cappello con garbo per dire all'oblio

che questa volta non potrà masticarti
né il suo coltello avrà oggi altra carne
se a tutti è nato un nuovo figlio immortale.

E nell'andarne, prendi una viola e gettala
ai flutti opachi del Lete. Avrà perduto ancora
per una gioia che non scorderai.

LETHE

Day or night, at that indefinite hour
when a solemn verse comes to life,
a true poem, whether by chance
or through the invention of an enemy in art

you need to purchase a red tie
and put on a linen suit, as was the custom
for the Lord's feast. With grace, then,
you will tip your hat, to convey to Oblivion

that this time he'll not chew you up
nor will his knife exact other flesh
for a new immortal child has been born unto all.

And as you leave, take a violet and cast it
into the opaque pools of Lethe. Who will have lost
yet again, for a joy you will not forget.

GIUGNO DI SICILIA

In questo buco caldo come l'alito di Dio
ora o controra persistono ubiqui nelle piazze
uomini e cani neri
prove di razze salate, di meticciato lungo
uomini intenti a logica e a millenni
di leggende che non perdono terra
neppure se fanno notte fonda
su concetti o su arguzie metafisiche.
Così femmine, madri e le cure loro
rimangono accidenti, puri sospetti
della ragione. Il sole insulta tutto
sbatte i salti dell'onda, scalfisce i denti
scolpisce palme esclamative e magre mentre
i fichi che crepano aborrati sulle rocce e le rocche
stillano sudori lenti e opachi dalla grana di carne.
Le zagare tardive e i gelsomini schiacciati
contro crete barocche, bianchi a sporcare bianchi,
attaccano la gola con un miele rancido d'oriente.
Niente di sacro sulle chiese dai fianchi inanellati
nella facciata cava, a nessun rito servono
capitelli di maschere e i pomi e gli ippogrifi
grigi di lava né i putti stolti che portano
a spalla l'acquasanta cavalcando delfini.
Per l'aria grave mormorano storie infinite
di fallanze veniali, tacciono le ragioni della vita
non quelle della morte.

Noto, Sicilia, 1998

SICILY IN JUNE

In this hole hot as the breath of God
at wake-time and nap-time everywhere in the piazzas
men and black dogs
endure, signs of seasoned races, of long
crossbreeding, men bent on logic and on millennia
of legends which give no ground
not even if they cast
abstractions and metaphysical nuance into deepest night.
So women, mothers, and their own cares
remain accidents for them, mere hunches
of the rational mind. The sun assaults
everything, slams the wave's surge, scrapes teeth,
carves the thin, exclamatory palm trees while
figs which burst straying down cliffs and fortresses
ooze slow, thick sweat as thick as meat.
Late orange and jasmine blossoms crushed
against baroque clays, white to stain white,
attack the throat with a rancid eastern honey.
Nothing's sacred on these churches with curlicued
flanks, with sunken façades. These capitals
of masks, fruits, and gray lava hippogriffs
serve no rite, nor do the foolish cherubs
shouldering holy water astride dolphins.
In dense air, they whisper infinite tales
of venial sins, hushing the reasons for life,
not the reasons for death.

Noto, Sicily, 1998

Translated by Rosanna Warren

PRECETTO DEL PROFETA

Traverserai la vita brano a brano
senza cani nel cuore senza artigli
e ti farai metronomo, segno del tempo, tempo
procederai col popolo dei te
di luna in lenta luna verso il mare
coprirai il monte, taglierai la piana
la sporta colma di fichi e olive
troverai bocche e braccia generose
non vorrai rive né avrai dove tornare.
Questi sono gli appunti che il tuo sangue
ha dettato per leggere la mappa dei sensi
e durare, incapace di ricordi
come il cipresso immane resta a Todi
folto d'anni e di bacche tegolate.

THE PROPHET'S PRECEPT

You will pass through life from scrap to scrap
no dogs in your heart, without claws
a metronome you will be, a marker of time, time
you will forge ahead leading your selves
seaward, from moon to sluggish moon,
you will cover the mountain, cross the plane
your basket brimming with figs and olives
generous lips and arms you will find
you will not want for shores
and have nowhere to return.
These are the notes your blood
has dictated, to help you read the map of the senses
and endure. Incapable of memory
like the awesome cypress of Todi,
abounding in years and trellised berries.

QUESITO

a Carlotta

Vogliamo rifare le mie nodose mani?
Vogliamo rifare terra e cielo
il mare più solenne e dolce il timo
vogliamo cambiare il sole, cambiare
il quadro nella stanza sul giardino,
vogliamo riprovare lenzuola di candido lino
rifare, amor mio, più sapido l'amare
perché le cose e i sensi tornino
a giocare ed ancora giocare un'altra vita?

QUESTION

for Carlotta

Shall we remake my gnarled hands?
Shall we remake the earth and sky,
make the sea more solemn, and sweeter thyme?
Shall we change the sun, change
the painting in the veranda,
again try sheets of sheer linen,
again, my love, spice up our love
to make our senses and world playful
again, to play once more at life?

DESERTO

Lo sanno anche i bambini
come nasce un deserto.
Non dipende dal sole
né dal morso ossessivo
delle formiche rosse,
di mosche dell'ulivo.

Un deserto si forma quando il cuore
degli uomini si fa pallido e secco
si forma se continuano a mancare
amore, ira o digiuno.
Così questo giardino
va stornando il suo verde
e finirà per logorarsi esusto
per sgarbi della pura indifferenza
per caduta dei venti di passione
per concorso dei nostri tanti senza.
E nessuno potrà un giorno scoprire
chi tra noi inferse il colpo decisivo.

DESERT

Even children know
how a desert is born.
It's not from the sun
or the relentless bite
of red ants,
of flies about the olive tree.

A desert forms when the hearts
of men wan and wither
if love, rage or hunger
stay in short supply.
And so does this garden
go bankrupt
its greenery parched
by the insults of sheer indifference
by faltering winds of passion
by the collusion of all our lacks.
And no one will someday discover
who between us delivered the final blow.

ETEROGENESI DEI FINI

Avrebbe voluto inventare
il mare generoso
e buone tutte
le difformi creature della terra,
farne fide nature
immerse nelle rose.
Avrebbe voluto creare
le volte in cielo pure
le molte, molte stelle
preziose e belle
per servire i cammini
e il fiorire del melo.
Avrebbe voluto che
brusco non rampollasse
lo starnuto che squinternò
le carte del progetto
le spinse quasi ad arte
in un imbuto lusco
sbaffando il segno lucido e perfetto
che si mutò in questo mondo indegno
dove a noi, gli errori,
rimase il solo officio
di compitare elenchi delle prove
e dei lugubri umori
del caso e dei destini.

BOTCHED PLANS

What He wanted was to make
the sea bountiful
and all the diverse creatures of the earth
good,
reliable forms
immersed in roses.
What He wanted was to create
celestial vaults
and the many, many stars
all precious and beautiful
to serve wayfarers
and the budding apple tree.
What He didn't want
was for a sudden sneeze
to explode and scatter
the pages of the plan
stuffing them artfully
down a clogged funnel
smudging every clear and perfect blueprint
only to yield this scornful world
whereby we, the mistakes
were left with the task
to compile the mounting evidence
the lists of fate and fortune's
mournful moods.

PARLANO CON SE STESSI

Parlano con se stessi, con i gatti e le res inanimatae
di molta voce occupano il silenzio che li opprime
a motti, a frasi rotte, a parate verbali sull'affondo
d'un interlocutore inesistente, organizzano
chiacchiera e argomento in domande e risposte
saltando ogni confine di ragione, ripetono, ripetono
in preda a pentimenti del pensiero e spinti
dal terrore di imporrire, di restare sepolti dalle assenze
da fughe di memoria, salutano per nome scarpe
e libri, pazienti. Sembrano incauti passeri di canto
intenti a segnalarsi anche al nemico. In verità
noi vecchi parliamo con noi stessi per essere ascoltati
al buio del giudizio. Quando il gelo s'accosta
ci scaldano nei suoni conosciuti soltanto
quei giochi di prestigio che possono ridurre
il silenzio a cosa umana. Meritiamo destino
se ancora lavoriamo la parola, misura d'esistenza.

TALKING TO THEMSELVES

They talk to themselves, with the cats and all that's inanimate
a surplus of voice occupies their oppressive silence
pat phrases, broken sentences, verbal skirmishes
with an absent interlocutor, gossip and disputes
alike organized according to question-and-answer
all reason shot to hell, as they repeat and repeat
prey to thoughts of repentance, driven
by terrors of putrefaction, of being buried by ghosts
by fugues of memory, they greet shoes
and books by name, patiently. Careless snowbirds
they seem, intent on warning even the enemy. In truth
we old folk talk to ourselves so as to be heard
in the darkness of judgment. When the cold closes in
all that warms us amid familiar sounds
are those magic tricks that can make of silence
something human. And we remain deserving of destiny
if still we manage to ply words, measure of existence.

DEL TEMPO

Qual tempo, quale mio onesto tempo più m'attende
del poco che mi resta? Conoscevo una volta
quanto costa la strada di un poeta. Pesto di colpi
come un lebbroso avvolto nelle bende, senza meta
prendeva le stradine di polvere, camminava a ritroso
buttandoci la vita, camminava e non poteva credere
alla favola tradita dell'amore, tra mine di rifiuto,
sassi di chi lo irride e austeri cardi del gran silenzio
batteva un tratturo sconnesso sognando la magia
di brave sfide e la grazia lucente del futuro.
Sempre ho scritto pensando di lasciare
la mia piccola lettera agli ignoti, un messaggio
nei vuoti di bottiglia che per l'onda riuscisse
a lambire la chiglia d'una barca di posteri. Ma ora
mi domando, ci aspetteranno posteri se in questo tempo
già non intravedo epigoni del mondo? Domando
se chi aspira all'assoluto rammenta bene
che, quante scorciatoie azzardi, sempre dovrà passare
il quotidiano che macchia ed unge indefettibilmente:
per il mito oggi è tardi. Posto il quesito cardine,
non mi rimane che pronunciare la frase di commiato
dalla gente, al termine delle commedie antiche: "Se tutto
è andato bene, plaudite a questo scherzo e con le mani
fate un gran frastuono". Andate figli, andate
con lo sguardo sorridente e raccontate
del mio tempo e di me, della radice, testardamente.

1998, senza patria nel tempo

OF TIME

What time, what earnest time yet awaits me
of the little that remains? I once knew
the toll demanded of a poet. Beaten,
battered like a bandaged leper, aimless,
he'd walk backward along dusty trails
expend his life, walking, in disbelief
at the betrayed fable of love, among minefields
of rejection, stones of derision, thistles of cosmic silence
he'd tread abandoned cattle-tracks dreaming of the magic
of righteous contests and futures of grace and light.
I've always written with the idea
of leaving a letter for someone unknown, a message
in a bobbing bottle that might graze the keel
of a boat of descendants. But now,
I ask, will posterity abide us if, already in this time of ours,
I picture no keepers of the world? I wonder
if those who crave the absolute recall,
no matter the number of shortcuts braved,
there's no way around the everyday
that never fails to stain and tarnish: today
it is too late for myth. Thus posed
the crucial question, all that's left for me
is to pronounce the same farewell
that closed the plays of old: "If all
went well, do acclaim this jest
and noisily clap your hands." Go, my children,
go with eyes smiling, and tell my story
and that of my time, of this root. Stubbornly.

1998, homeless in Time

DICE IL MERCANTE

Sei niente, niente. I versi zoppi,
i tuoi scazonti, sono niente. Non puoi certo
mangiarli né ti danno per altra via

da vivere, nessuno li può usare
come leva o per mare, da farmaco,
da stocco. Utili a chi, utili a che?

Sono soltanto prova di neghittosi geni,
antenne per segnali convulsi, gagliardetti
di latta, pinnacoli che confondono

i giochi della sorte, che annunciano
la morte. Non servono a niente,
come non serve la perfida allegria

di Mozart, il discorso sull'ente e sul non ente,
un ossimoro o il pianto d'una madre,
come i colori del tramonto alpino, il canto

d'un bambino e le fusa del gatto.
Così non serve un matto che si ferma
e farnetica agli astanti perplessi.

SO SAYS THE MERCHANT

You are nothing, nothing. Your lame verses,
your rhymes, are nothing. Surely
you cannot eat them, nor do they otherwise

earn your keep, no one can use them
as lever or sail, as medicine
or sword. Good for whom, then, for what?

They are but proof of listless genes,
antennae for convulsive signals, pennants
of tin, pinnacles that confuse

the moves of fate, and only herald
death. They serve no purpose,
useless as the wicked andantes of Mozart

as any discourse on being and non-being,
as oxymorons or a mother's cry,
as the colors of an alpine sunset, the song

of a child or the purr of a cat.
Likewise we have no use for madmen
who stop and rant at baffled bystanders.

PIAZZA NAVONA

In memoria di Gino Bonichi (in arte, Scipione), ultimo
pittore di Roma barocca, morto di tisi nel 1933
all'età di 29 anni, come aveva predetto un monaco spagnolo

Quella sera la tua pazienza mistica
gettò il guanto alla cruda primavera
e abbandonò i pennelli dolci e biondi.
Il petto sputò tutto il sangue caldo
in faccia al cielo di Piazza Navona
che prese fuoco
e di quel fuoco avvolse fondi e chiese
guglie, fontane e case.
Lasciò illese di biacca
le code dei tritoni e le conchiglie
perché le trombe dell'apocalisse
tuonassero più forte.
Tutto era stato detto a Collepardo
dal presagio spagnolo della morte.
E tu incendiasti Roma.
E Roma ricordando, ancora brucia.

PIAZZA NAVONA

In memory of Gino Bonichi (in art Scipione),
Rome's last baroque painter, who died of consumption
in 1933, at 24, as foretold by a Spanish monk.

That evening your mystical patience
flung its glove at the brutal spring
and left behind its gentle blond brushes.
Hot blood spat up from your chest
in the face of the Piazza Navona sky
that caught fire
fire that swept backdrops and churches
steeples, fountains and homes.
Leaving untouched the flake white
of seashells and tails of tritons
for the trumpets of the apocalypse
to thunder evermore.
All had been foretold at Collepardo
by a Spanish omen of death.
And you ignited Rome.
And Rome, remembering, still burns.

L'ESPRIT DE LA LOI

Il regno della legge
è un chiaroscuro indegno
un grottesco di vicoli e di ponti
dal disegno sottile e periglioso
creato dalle astuzie dei suoi autori—
le cosiddette arguzie delle fonti.
È un miraggio agitato
dai malditesta e i rari buonumori
di volubili interpreti pei quali
ogni sentenza è festa.

L'ESPRIT DE LA LOI

The kingdom of law
is a flawed chiaroscuro
a grotesque array of alleys and bridges
intricate and perilous in the design
of its cagey creators—
the so-called witticisms of sources.

It is a mirage fuelled
by the migraines and rare good spirits
of moody interpreters for whom
every sentence is a feast.

LA QUESTIONE MORALE

Tra il bene e il male
non ci sono frontiere
                    né avvisi d'una marca.
C'è un povero animale
                    intento a bere
a fottere
            e morire piano piano
una bestiola armata della mano
cui la stazione eretta suggerì
di guardare lontano
e all'ora dei tramonti
rifare i conti con cuore febbrile.

MORAL ISSUE

Between good and evil
there are no frontiers
                    or commercial breaks.
There's a poor animal
                    busy drinking
fucking
        and slowly dying
a little beast with a hand for a weapon
whose erect posture
extended his field of vision
and who everyday at sunset
feverishly takes stock anew.

LA BITTA

E un giorno, figli miei, vidi che ne partiste
colmi di libri, di guasti ereditati e d'allegrie
libere navi che salpavano a mete sconosciute.
Io lì nel porto, sul porto, vi ammirai scomparire
senza sapervi seguire neppure con la mente
mentre scrutavo il solco delle scie e il fumo
delle vostre sigarette che imitavano ardenti ciminiere.
Tenni il confine come una bitta bruna che non veglia
boghe o sartie né gomene e gasse. A volte
mi sembrò che tornaste a vicini ripari sfilando
davanti la mia costa più in basso della linea
d'orizzonte. Forse, fu di notte e di brume ma
non vidi scafo che gettò le cime ad ancorarsi,
ad abbracciare il ferro sul bordo della banchina vecchia.
Forse, soltanto non vi riconobbi.

THE BOLLARD

And came the day, my children, when I saw you leave
saddled with books, with inherited scars and cheer
ships free to set sail for unknown arrivals.
There, from the pier, on the dock, I watched you disappear
unable to track you even with my mind
while I eyed the furrows in the water and the smoke
of your cigarettes burning like chimneystacks.
Me, I marked the boundary, a brown bollard
who won't keep watch over bogues, riggings, ropes and knots.
There were times, I thought, when you'd return
to take refuge, as you hugged the coastline beneath my horizon.
Perhaps, but it was nighttime and misty, and I saw
no ship cast anchor, no ropes wrapped
around the iron on the old wharf. Or perhaps
I simply failed to recognize you.

SCACCO MATTO

(11 settembre 2001)

Sono nato a Rockaway, sotto Brooklyn, in un lembo
di terra che sembra un dito largo e teso nell'Atlantico.
Non ricordo donna che m'abbia custodito d'amore
l'infanzia e i primi incanti. Ma è stato bello crescere
dietro una siepe, ogni giorno l'oceano negli occhi, bello
come scovare orgoglio malnascosto nella faccia italiana
di mio padre la volta in cui entrai a casa con il primo
stipendio da contabile. Volle giocare una partita a scacchi
e fumando due sole sigarette, fece che lo battessi senza scuse
su una mossa di torre e di regina. Concluse che dovevo
sempre stare attento alle torri, comunque infide nei loro
movimenti lunghi su un percorso di croce bianco e nero.

"Infide", disse serio il mio vecchio e ricordavo la parola
sorridendo di martedì quell'undici settembre mentre
correvo a lavorare per Manhattan.
E il suo monito posso riconoscere
ora che sono polvere dispersa da un lampo osceno
polvere abbandonata fra altre polveri scomposte sotto
un marciapiede divelto, a fianco della foglia dove
mio padre non potrà mai trovarmi nemmeno
per tenermi la mano degli scacchi. Ero di Rockaway
e non ho avuto amore né conforto di donna
una adesso ne venga e chieda agli iris bianchi
di fiorire nel nome mio nascosto, cancellato.

CHECKMATE

(September 11, 2001)

I was born in Rockaway, below Brooklyn, on a strip
of land that looks like a fat finger stretching into the Atlantic.
I remember no woman who cherished my cradle or teenage
awe. And yet, it was special to grow up behind a hedge,
with the ocean every day in my eyes, special
to uncover the pride my father's Italian face couldn't hide
the time I brought home my first paycheck as a CPA.
He wanted to play chess and, smoking but two cigarettes,
let me beat him unequivocally,
on a combination rook-and-queen. He ended
by saying to always watch out for those treacherous towers
and the black-and-white crosses their long moves plot.

"Treacherous," my old man said, somberly: I remembered the word
with a smile that Tuesday, September 11,
as I raced to work through Manhattan.
And I recall his warning now
that I am dust scattered by an obscene blast
dust lost among the dusts of others undone
below a ravaged sidewalk, next to the leaf where
never will my father find me not even
to hold the hand I'd use to play chess. I came from Rockaway
where I knew no woman's love or warmth
may one now come and ask the white irises
to bloom in my name, hidden, erased.

NUOVI MITI

Il toro dei destini, tonante e inarrestabile vola fra i cieli
d'Asia e li ravvolge. Trascina in cerchio un altro rapimento
e sparge al vento sangue e senno, onore, pietà e riti.
Rovescia i nuovi miti sugli animali umani, sugli stessi fratelli
adesso vinti adesso vincitori che al suo passaggio giacciono indistinti
e abbandonati come cani sotto il raggio del sole, senza dèi da implorare
senza pane né vie dove muovere passi per la fuga, senza lutto.
Negati a tutto negano l'esistenza con i denti, deflagrano la propria
e l'altrui vita in brandelli e minuzzoli di carne da ritornare
in polvere dispersa.
        È il toro delle stragi universali, il toro che frantuma
specchio e tempio, che versa figlia e madre ai fili d'erba
mescolando questa poltiglia astratta di fedi e storie, di bandiere
e colori della pelle, di bestie al bando, di latte e d'uva, d'arti e di sapere.
E resta sull'asfalto un mare d'ombre
nei tramonti d'oriente.

NEW MYTHS

The bull of destinies, thundering, reckless, soars
ravaging Asian skies, dragging in its swirl another rape,
sowing in the wind blood and reason, rituals, mercy and honor.
Spilling new myths on human animals, brothers in turn vanquished
and victors, left lying forsaken in its wake
like sun-drenched dogs with no gods to beseech, with neither bread
nor escape, with no chance to mourn. Bereft,
they deny with their teeth all that exists, detonate life, their own,
of others, into bits and tatters of flesh to revert
into a flutter of dust.

      It is the bull of universal slaughters, the bull that shatters
mirror and temple, that returns mother and daughter to grassy fields
in an abstract mixture of faiths and histories, of flags and races,
of banished beasts, of milk and grapes, arts and wisdom.
Leaving on the asphalt a sea of shadows
across Eastern sunsets.

PROTOCOLLI DI GUERRA
(Bagdad non è lontana)

a Titos Patrikios

Di questo tempo
non farai memorie per la tua fame eterna.
Non vedi quante scorie
nello stame tra cui affonda la carne dei viventi,
non vedi che la scatola e i cassetti
dove abbondano argenti del passato
non potrebbero accogliere né confetti né valve
da un presente fondato sul gesso dei commerci,
perduto a contemplarsi dallo specchio
in cui cerca se stesso tra le stanze del mondo?
Non t'avvedi che per la prima volta
ogni umano edifica rovine per gli eredi
decretando i più stupidi protocolli di guerra
mentre il futuro serra i suoi battenti
perché sia celebrata sull'altare statistico
la gloria di marionette assenti, agite
dal puro nulla, sorte e fiorite
in mezzo al campo amaro dell'oblio?
Di questo tempo non farai memorie.

PROTOCOLS OF WAR
(Baghdad is not far)

for Titos Patrikios

Of this time you'll gather no memories
for your eternal hunger.
Can't you see the slags in the weave
that enfolds the flesh of the living?
Can't you see that the boxes and drawers
where the silver of bygone days abounds
have no room for trinkets or seashells
of a present founded on plaster markets,
lost gazing at itself in the mirror
seeking itself in the halls of the world?
Don't you see that for the first time
every man erects ruins for his heirs
enacting inane protocols of war
while the future slams its shutters tight
so as to celebrate on statistical altars
the glory of mindless marionettes
maneuvered by nothingness,
sprung in the bitter fields of oblivion?
Of this time you'll gather no memories.

LA LUNA E L'ONDA

Mentre la prima luna s'alza in trono
occhi sui vivi, col pallore e lo scherno
d'una vecchia pastiglia consumata,
il passeraccio solo e imbalonato
dall'egra tamerice guarda al mare—
azul y azul, inmenso azul redondo—
guarda al di là di dune e di barene
con un occhio soltanto l'altro in sonno,
trepidante per prendere la mira
dell'onda definita e trionfante
che nessun colpo potrà mai fermare
sul confine del sogno che viviamo.
Quell'onda che avanzando ci costringe
e senza requie ci fa domandare
perché io, io chi, io quando
ed io per quanto ancora?
Ma la luna procede verso il cielo
che livido s'imbruna
testimone impassibile e solenne
sull'affanno del nulla.

THE MOON AND THE WAVE

As the early moon is enthroned,
eyes upon the living, pale and wizened
as a thinned lozenge,
the old buzzard, oafish and alone
from the scrawny tamarisk beholds the sea—
azul y azul, inmenso azul redondo—
looks beyond the dunes and shoals
with only one eye, the other, sleepy,
flitting, to take aim of the one
precise, triumphant wave
that no shot ever will stop
at the edge of the dream we inhabit.
Wave whose onslaught compels us
relentlessly to ask
why me, me who, me when
and for how much longer?
And the moon ascends
the wounded sky of dusk
a witness, solemn and unmoved
over the weary weight of the void.

LA FARFALLA BREVE

"Non v'accorgete voi che noi siam vermi
nati a formar l'angelica farfalla?"
—Dante Alighieri, Purg.X, 124-25

Se non si può tentare più avventura
né fabbricare a mano altri ricordi
forse l'unica, vera impresa umana
consisterà nell'ignorare il tempo
senza rispetto
e voltate le spalle, resistere nel sogno.
Escluso in questo modo ogni conflitto
fra l'inizio e la necessaria fine
resterà ignoto il vincolo del vuoto
transito nostro.
Come sa fare la farfalla breve.

THE SHORT-LIVED BUTTERFLY

"Can you not see that we are worms, each one
born to become the Angelic butterfly?"
—Dante Alighieri, *Purgatory X, 124-125*

If all adventure is now foreclosed
and there are no more memories to fashion by hand
perhaps the only, truly human quest
will consist in paying time no mind
no respect
and, backs turned, resisting in the dream.
Thus severed every conflict
between the beginning and necessary end,
the link of this empty transit of ours
will remain unknown.
As does the short-lived butterfly.

COME LE MARGHERITE

Perficere la vita non si può.
Solo il vento del caso
ci rovescia trascorsi ed inconclusi
come le margherite di stagione
al termine del tempo
e in un lampo ci porta a compimento
in un lampo consuma la radice
e ogni minima traccia
di lamento.

LIKE THE DAISIES

There's no perfecting life.
Only the winds of chance
upend us, weathered and unfulfilled
like daisies
at season's end,
and in a flash convey us to completion
in a flash undo the root
and every slightest trace
of sorrow.

IO NACQUI

I

Milioni d'anni fa nelle valli del Rift
radi gli alberi ormai della savana arsa dal sole
levai un giorno le zampe dalla terra
a nutrirmi del poco verde e dei frutti rimasti.
Nel tempo e fra le trappole del caso,
quelle zampe che s'alzavano al cielo—
provando e riprovando—si misero ad ardire
un'altra vita per i figli dei figli dei miei figli
lungo innumeri stirpi.
E si fecero brave nel cacciare e combattere
nell'esplorare la natura e la femmina
nel difendere e bere, nel trasportare figli
e prede in salvo. Si fecero fide compagne
in cerca d'altre terre.
Ma mentre l'era procedeva lenta nell'alternanza
di gelo e disgelo, fra dispersioni, salti, tetti e abissi
quelle appendici si mutarono in mani,
soli artigli capaci di comporre offerte e sacrifici
per bussare alle presunte porte degli dei
mani sempre al servizio dell'offesa
contro gli altri viventi
e della misteriosa fantasia che armò
la selce colorata e dette fuoco alla caverna
tracciando puri segni di fieri combattenti,
alci e bisonti.
Dal sangue di mille risse il mio io nacque.
E così fino ad oggi
ancora vive e muore ogni altro io.

MY BIRTH

I

Millions of years ago in the valleys of the Rift
amid a smatter of trees on the sun-drenched savannah,
one day I raised my paws from the earth
to feed from what leaves and fruits were left.
In time, in-between the traps of chance
those outstretched paws that scraped the sky—
reaching, time and time again—began to brave
another life for the children of my children's children,
down through countless generations.
And they learned expertly to hunt and fight
to explore nature and the female
to defend and drink, to lead to safety offspring
and prey alike. Becoming trusty partners
in search of other lands.
But while the ages took turns slowly icing and thawing
across scatterings, hurdles, rooftops and depths
those appendages mutated into hands
the only claws capable of offerings and sacrifices
meant to knock at the presumed gates of gods
hands ever in the service
of offending other beings
and of the mysterious fantasy that armed
colorful flints, igniting the walls of caves
tracing pure signs of proud combatants,
of elks and bison.
From the blood of a thousand skirmishes was I born.
And so on, until today,
as every other I lives and dies.

II

L'ultima glaciazione incatenava la tundra delle terre d'occidente
percorse e dominate dal bue muschiato, dal mammuth, dall'orso
da cavalli del pelo e da bisonti, da lupi e volpi, da feroci predatori
    del gelo.
E sulla desolata piattaforma che si sarebbe nominata Europa
trentamila anni prima del presente, fra Otranto e Circeo, fra
    Dordogna
e Cantabrico, tra Pirenei ed Ardèche, si aggiravano gli homines
    sapientes
i primi Cro Magnon, pel resto inermi, muniti solo di trapezi in selce
di coltelli di pietra, aghi di schegge d'osso, arpioni e rozze lance
forgiate con i femori di renna, strumenti astuti, prove di sapienza da
    brandire
nelle notti e nei giorni sempre afflitti dalla necessità di essere ancora.
Le loro stesse mani, pur immerse tra i ghiacci e lo sgomento del buio
e del silenzio, si indussero a impugnare spezzati di ematite e d'ocra
    gialla,
iridescenti gessi di argille, carbone tratto dal bruciar dei legni, ad
    impugnare
utensili di roccia per graffire e inondare di colore gli anditi di riparo
mutandoli in santuari ove cantare lo stupore del mondo e i desideri
con tutto il culto della devozione alle prede di vita, femmina od alce.
E l'immaginazione celebrò trionfi e rotte di animali in fuga e le
    ossessive
immagini vulvari dentro le grotte di Cussac e Chauvet, di Les Eyzies,
    di Lascaux,
di Pech Merle, e così usando di bulini e lime, di scalpelli e gradine,
    quelle mani

II

It was when the last ice age imprisoned the western tundras
overrun and ruled by the mammoth and musk ox, by bears, bison
and shaggy horses, by foxes and wolves, and fierce predators of the
    frost.
It was then, across the desolate land later named Europe
thirty thousand years before now, between Otranto and Circeo,
    Dordogne
and Cantabrico, between the Pyrenees and Ardèche, that homo
    sapiens roamed,
the first Cro-Magnon, harmless, fitted only with trapezoid flints
and stone knives, needles of splintered bone, harpoons and clumsy
    lances
hewn from the femurs of reindeer, savvy instruments, forms of
    knowledge
to brandish in nights and days forever hounded by the urge to go on
    being.
Those very hands, frostbit and sunken in the harrows of darkness
and silence, pushed to grip nuggets of hematite and yellow ochre,
iridescent chalks of clay, of burnt wood, pushed
to grip tools of stone, to etch and flood with color their caves
turned sanctuaries, where to sing desire and the wonders of the
    world,
devoted to the cult of all of life's preys, of elk and woman.
Thus were celebrated the triumphs and flights of animals, the
    images of vulval
obsession at Cussac and Chauvet, at Les Eyzies, Lascaux, and Pech
    Merle.
And in the use of burins and chisels, of rasps and files, those hands

composero in un minimo di avorio la Venere feconda di Lespugue
e la casta Signora del cappuccio, battute prime che aprirono il
   concerto di nascita
dell'arte e dello spirito, uniche gratuità concesse all'uomo dalla
   raggiunta
natura sua di bestia ormai imperfetta.

composed in a sliver of ivory the fertile Venus of Lespugue
and the chaste Hooded Lady, opening notes of the inaugural
    concert
of the birth of art and spirit, lone concessions made to man
and his accomplished nature of long-imperfect beast.

ORATORIO

(Madrid 11 marzo 2004)

Famiglia mia, uomini del mondo
donne, bambini del mondo
da qualche tempo abbiamo cominciato
a morire scoppiando all'improvviso
frantumati
come bersagli presi al centro
da un deflagrante e povero insensato
che nel nome asserito del suo dio
va lavorando alla fine della carne
in cielo, in terra, in mare, in ogni luogo
ed ha fretta di ritornare polvere
pur di ridurre nella stessa polvere
non il solo nemico ma anche gli altri
i qualunque di noi folti viandanti
come nessuna bestia fece mai
per tutta la memoria della terra.
Allora, famiglia mia, uomini del mondo
donne, bambini del mondo, cerchiamo
di capire che qui non gioca il fatto
che ciascuno di noi deve arrendersi
al caso e alla sua arte millenaria, ilare
quando sceglie le prede fra gli umani,
ma si tratta di fare l'abitudine
al gesto fosco di animali nuovi,
mutazioni d'una creatura resa fuori stirpe
e abbandonata a una continua semina di offese
che arriva a praticare orrore e morte

ORATION

(Madrid, March 11, 2004)

My family, men of the world
women, children of the world
for some time now we've taken
to dying by suddenly exploding
shattered
like bull's-eyes blasted
by some poor, detonating madman
working for the demise of the flesh
in the presumed name of his god,
in heaven, on earth, at sea, everywhere
in a rush to return unto dust
reducing to that selfsame dust
not only the enemy but the rest as well,
the clusters of us everymen.
In ways no other beast has ever done
for as long as the earth can remember.
Thus, my family, men of the world
women, children of the world, let us try
to understand that what's at stake
is not our individual surrender
to chance and its ageless, fanciful art
of choosing its everyday human prey
but our ability to become accustomed
to the grim habits of new animals,
mutations of a creature who's left the fold
run amok to sow contempt
to wield horror and death

giudicati talmente necessari
da doverli portare alla rinfusa
contro i loro già simili abiurati.
E così a giusto e ingiusto, colpevole
o innocente, amico e ostile, impuro
o penitente. Sono esseri lucifughi,
votati al nulla, scomposti dalla storia
e dal maligno stormire delle stelle
che strisciano ad oriente in cerca d'oro,
esseri pervenuti all'abisso insondato
d'un rancore vorace e tanto fondo
da negarli perfino
a quell'istinto di sopravvivenza
che comuna ogni specie
e regge sia gli arieti del covile
che le feroci belve di savana.
Quindi famiglia mia, uomini
del mondo, donne nostre regine,
questo rebus non si potrà lasciare
alle speciose demenze di potenti e reggitori
ma si impone gravoso alle coscienze
dei popoli sottili e solleva ai filosofi
qualche questione in più di quelle astate
nei secoli dei secoli intorno ai fini
e alle ragioni dell'umano seme,
della sua perduranza.
Nel frattempo, noi uomini del mondo
noi i quisque, noi fratelli inermi
fratelli della norma, gente del pane
seguitiamo, vi prego, a camminare per le terre
ed a fendere il coraggioso mare,

essential weapons
in a random game of warfare
against the already disowned of kin.
Against just and unjust alike, guilty
or innocent, friend or foe, impure
or pious. Lucifugue beings
devoted to nothingness, dismantled by history
and the evil rustling of stars
slouching eastward in search of gold,
beings at the brink of an unfathomed abyss
of rancor so boundless as to negate
the very instinct to survive
that binds every species,
and sustains alike the rams in the pen
and the savannah's wild beasts.
And so my family, men
of the world, women our queens,
this riddle cannot be left
to the mindlessness of those in power
but confronts the good conscience
of people everywhere, raising new questions
even for our philosophers, above and beyond
the age-old debates around
the presence and purpose
of man on earth.
Meanwhile, we men of the world,
we triflings, we unarmed brothers
brothers of the norm, people of bread
let us continue to walk the earth
and brave the seas,
let us try to comprehend and even ablate

proviamo a comprendere e ad ablare
cause del male inferto
fasciati dalla forza del sorriso
noi, coltivatori della creazione
quotidiani pastori di utopie
perseveranti l'arte di sognare,
noi seguitiamo
senza curarci del fetido soffio
che ci vorrebbe presi dal sospetto
di pensare ed amare inutilmente
di fare figli solo perché siano
gratuiti bersagli da squarciare,
insomma, portatori sani
dell'assoluto niente.

the causes of the harm inflicted,
to forbid such evil from now on,
bandaged in the strength of our smiles
we, who cultivate creation
we ordinary shepherds of utopia
who persevere in the art of dreaming
let us continue
indifferent to the fetid whiff
that would move us to wonder
why we even think and love
why have children
if not to make of them
gratuitous targets of savagery
healthy carriers, ultimately
of nothingness.

"OPERAZIONE FAMIGLIA MEDICI"
(dalla stampa dell'11.4.2004)

Dice che esumeranno
quasi cinquanta corpi di quei Medici
che così a lungo tennero in governo
la Toscana e parlarono col mondo.
Dice che questa indagine
sulle spoglie dei nobili defunti
sia un fatto molto atteso dagli storici.
Dice che per due anni
intendenti e patologi affannati
studieranno quanto rimane,
per capire stili di vita e cause di morte.
Però si tace il fatto
che questa operazione di disturbo
servirà unicamente a storici, patologi e intendenti
per provare occasioni di esistenza
e, di risulta, consumare postume vendette
alle ceneri di Savonarola. In verità
in questo nostro travagliato mondo
basterebbero le prove di sinistro e tetro gusto
offerte dai brandelli dei corpi allineati
in fondo alla cappella granducale
in teche di cristallo e reliquiari.
Si mediti.
Nonostante tutta la gloria e tanto grande fama,
nonostante magnificenza e privilegi dati
alle lettere, all'arte ed alle scienze che mai
hanno avuto il pari lungo i secoli, neppure

OPERATION MEDICI

(from press reports dated April 11, 2004)

Word is they're to exhume
nearly fifty corpses of the Medici family
who for so long held sway
over Tuscany, and conversed with the world.
Word is that tests
on those noble remains
are eagerly awaited by historians.
Word is that for two years
anxious experts and pathologists
will study what's left
to ascertain lifestyles and causes of death.
What gets hushed, however,
is that this bothersome exercise
will only avail historians, pathologists and experts
to probe chance existences
and, as a result, to avenge
the ashes of Savonarola. In truth
in this forlorn world of ours
the sinister and macabre taste exhibited
by bits of bodies all lined up
at the far end of the grand duke's chapel
in see-through shrines and reliquaries
ought to have sufficed.
Or so you'd think.
Notwithstanding all the glory and fame,
the grandeur and privileges bestowed
on the arts and letters and sciences

si riesce a stare in pace sotto un pezzo
di marmo dopo mezzo millennio dalla fine.
Perché una mano di boiardi arriva
a risbaldire nel frugarti le vesti funerarie,
pungendoti la spina che rimane
per sbranarsi l'indizio di un peccato
come un babà di Caflish.
Allora altro non resta da concludere.
È meglio cancellare le tracce del passaggio
alla maniera d'un indiano in fuga
e giù oscuro a confondersi
nella fossa comune.
Non basta più proteggersi la vita
ci dobbiamo salvare anche la morte.

and never equaled in the course of centuries,
there's still no resting in peace, not even under
a slab of marble, half a millennium later.
All because a boyar's hand
will cop a feel under your sepulchral dress
to prick what's left of your spine
and hungrily tear at a sign of sin
as if at a rum-soaked baba.
There's nothing left, then, other to conclude
that it's better to erase all traces of passage
in the manner of an Indian in flight, and to be obscured
in the morass of a pauper's grave.
It no longer suffices to protect one's life,
we now need also to preserve our death.

IL GESTO

Adesso, ancora adesso mi sorprende
il marinaio che ripetendo il gesto da millenni
s'alza in mezzo alla barca appena il primo sole
di una qualunque Delo gli accarezza la spalla
fa un pezzo di bravura contro il cielo
e accupola la rete che si smorza lentissima
sull'onda e in trasparenze affonda
verso le mete di pescame e d'alghe,
verso le udienze delle pie sirene.

THE GESTURE

Again, yet again does the seaman
surprise me, repeating the age-old gesture
of standing in the middle of the boat no sooner
than the dawn of a new Delos grazes his shoulder
the sky a showcase for his skill
as he twirls a net that slowly slips rounded
into the waves and dips to its destination
unto swarms of fish and seaweed
unto the chambers of godly sirens.

CON NESSUNO

Giunto alle sere in cui
è facile contare sulle dita
le prossime stagioni
e mi raggiunge l'adito del cuore
l'urrù delle colombe innamorate
ho dalla mia una nuova libertà
di parlare col mondo impunemente
conquistandomi al peggio la patente
dell'anziano irascibile e insensato.
Posso provare
il liberale brivido quietista
d'una franchezza
che da nessuno sarà mai chiamata
a fare i propri conti con nessuno
e riparando in solidi silenzi
scamperà ad ogni debito di replica
e al fittume delle interrogazioni senza gloria.

A NEW FREEDOM

Having reached that evening hour
when you can count on the fingers of one hand
the seasons that remain
and discern the reasons of the heart
the flutter of doves in heat
I've a new freedom
to speak my mind, unfettered
acquiring, at worst, the reputation
of a senseless and irritable old man.
This affords me
the liberal quietist quiver
of the kind of frankness
for which I'll never have to answer
left with no scores to settle
from which to retreat into dense silences
owing no one the honor of a reply.
Spared the spittle of further interrogation.

IL CAPRO DEL SILENZIO

Hai passato la vita
a scusarti di esistere con tutti
a nascondere il cuore e gli altri frutti
a intimidirti come una smarrita
per i bravi talenti che la luna
t'ha dato senza cura di ferita
quando ha fatto il bagaglio di te stesso.
Senza avvisarti d'essere per questo
il bersaglio del raglio generale
il capro del più basso saturnale
preferito dal caravanserraglio dei pidocchi,
uno sbaglio per gli occhi e per la mente—
barbaglio da negare
quantomeno per mezzo del silenzio.

SCAPEGOAT OF SILENCE

You've gone through life
apologizing to everyone for existing
hiding your heart and other fruits
like a lost soul ashamed
of the earnest talents bestowed on you
by the moon when, heedless of the wounds
inflicted, it made you who you are.
Forgetting, however, to warn you
that still you'd become everyone's fall guy
a saturnalian scapegoat
a patsy for lecherous lice
eyesore and mindsore—
rather, effulgence disavowed
by the silence that surrounds you.

I FANTI DEL COMMERCIO

"For poetry makes nothing happen . . ."
—W. H. Auden, "In Memory of W. B. Yeats"

C'è chi ha scritto in un verso impudico
che l'arte non fa mai accadere niente.
Lo scrisse un bardo—il più sano di mente,
il miglior cuore fra gli amici in gioco—
e credo l'abbia fatto con destrezza
per irridere i fanti del commercio.
Tu dissenti, tu comunque ribatti ad alta voce
che l'arte fa accadere la bellezza.

Ma quando bellezza accade,
una sfera di fuoco piove da cielo a terra
ilare e devastante come l'ira di Giove.
Rovescia oggetti della devozione, rovescia
tomba e melo la bellezza, trasporta serre
e rose della vita nei più remoti lidi e per millenni.
Così l'arte trasforma i gridi in canti,
il male in alti pianti di tragedia
rende feconde pene della storia
conquista la memoria e la consola
nelle donne e nei figli.

Se al tramonto che ruggisce sul Tevere in aprile
scoppia basso un cespuglio di rondini
e s'allontana diramando in arco,

THE KNAVES OF COMMERCE

"For poetry makes nothing happen . . ."
—W. H. Auden, *"In Memory of W. B. Yeats"*

As a shameless verse would have it
art never makes anything happen.
So wrote a bard—the sanest of friends,
the truest heart to play this game—
and so he did, I'd say, with artistry
to scoff at the knaves of commerce.
You, however, dissent, and counter out loud
that art makes beauty happen.

But when beauty happens
a sphere of fire rains down from heaven
as rowdy and ruinous as Jupiter's ire.
Upending objects of devotion, upending
tomb and apple tree, beauty sweeps life's gardens
and greenhouses to faraway shores, for millennia on end.
And so does art turn shouts into song,
evil into noble tears of tragedy,
render bounteous the sorrows of history
and conquer memory, later consoled
in women and our children.

If an April sunset roaring over the Tiber
explodes a shrub of low-flying swallows
scattered in the form of a tended bow,

l'arte genera dunque la bellezza
e la bellezza quei costanti amori
riflessi dalla perenne semina del vento.
Allora
l'arte è la sola opera umana
che sa creare
oltre il limite scarso d'ogni tempo.

art then does generate beauty
and beauty in turn those steadfast loves
reflected in the endless sowing of the wind.
Art, then,
is the sole human craft
able to create
beyond the feeble limit of every age.

QUALI BARBARI

"Che aspettiamo, raccolti nella piazza?
Oggi arrivano i barbari."
—Konstantinos Kavafis

Non calano dai monti dei Balcani
tracce umane ignorate dalla storia
né abbandonano più remote sponde
per affrontare il mare, aggrovigliati
come resti dell'ultimo pescame
su carrette sospinte dai respiri.
Se appena a terra vanno praticando
costumi ignoti e differenti riti
se balbettano per idiomi astrusi
se hanno altri colori della pelle
e ti chiedono pane per la strada
trascinando le lacere creature
a cui ogni cane abbaia,
non sono quelli i barbari, puoi credermi.

I barbari
vivono in sonno dentro ad ogni uomo
latenti e armati abitano anche in voi
se ne stanno acquattati in mezzo al cuore
dei più miti compagni e dei fratelli
dei miei adorati figli e dei nipoti.
La barbarie s'accartoccia nei corpi
nascosta fra grovigli e gangli oscuri

WHAT BARBARIANS

"What are we waiting for, gathered in the square?
Today the barbarians arrive."
—Constantine Cavafy

They don't descend from Balkan highlands
human vestiges ignored by history
nor do they abandon faraway shores
to brave the sea entangled
like fish left over from the day's last catch
on rickety boats that run on sighs.
If, upon landing, you see them practice
strange customs and alien rituals
if they babble in baffling tongues
or wear a skin of a different color
begging for bread on the street
dragging along frayed children
who rouse the bark of every dog,
believe me, they are not the barbarians.

The barbarians
lie asleep inside every man
idle but armed they inhabit us all,
you too, crouched in the hearts
of even the meekest of friends and kin
of my own beloved children and grandchildren.
Barbarism takes root in the body
buried, knotted in murky ganglia

langue nel nostro sangue e al primo nulla
punge e ispina sia l'ossa che la vena
esce rabbiosa e va rasente i muri
a procurare pena con la mossa
d'una violenza appresa nella culla
quando impastiamo l'anima nel buio
coltivando il talento da rapace
sull'esempio di pessimi maestri.

Barbara è questa carne universale
che nasce al male dalla nostra carne.

it languishes in our blood and at the slightest nothing
it pricks and enthorns both bone and vein
gushes forth with rage and slithers along walls
to wreak sorrow, with the mark
of violence acquired in our cribs
when we knead our soul in the dark
and feed our predatory knack
emulating the worst of our teachers.

Barbaric is this universal flesh
born unto evil from this, our flesh.

OSPITI

Gli occhi di questa casa lungo Ripa
si ostinano sul fiume
che procede caracollando
per onde e strie di melme verdibrune
e più celere appare dagli squarci
nel fogliame dei platani concordi
che ci affrontano armati di alabarde
come grigi guerrieri marezzati
beccheggiando alla cima sotto il vento.
Ci scherniscono i passeri dai rami.

Siamo ospiti, mia donna, non possiamo
ignorarlo. Ospiti a pagamento nel pensiero
ospiti nei ricordi, tollerati. In prestito
l'amare, in prestito ogni storia traversata
e la nuvola che balla allegra
nel cielo di giacinto
malgrado la presenza degli dèi.
Prendemmo in uso transitorio
il pianto per i visi perduti nei cassetti
in uso colpe e affanni reperiti per via, in uso
la scena madre al freddo d'un lampione
e la soglia di estatica emozione
che sfioriamo senza capire
contemplando la Maestà di Piero.
Puri accidenti da rendere alla svelta
quinte precarie come l'acqua viola dell'Egeo

GUESTS

The eyes of our home along the Tiber
stay fixed on the river
as it bounces and breaks
in rapids and streaks of greenish-brown slime
its sweep all the faster when viewed
between the leaves of the orderly sycamores
that face us armed with halberds
like grey marbled warriors
staggering on treetops under the wind.
And from the branches sparrows scoff at us.

We are guests, my lady, let us
not forget. Guests in thought for a fee
guests of memories, indulged. On loan
our love, on loan every affair we cross
and the cloud that dances merrily
in the hyacinth sky
despite the presence of the gods.
Borrowed were the tears
cried for faces now lost in drawers
borrowed the guilt and anguish found along the way,
the crucial scene in the cold air of a street lamp
and the threshold of ecstatic feeling
chanced upon but never seized
in our contemplation of Piero's Majesty.
Sheer mishaps to be returned on demand
scenes improvised like the purple Aegean

che felici ci accolse nel crepuscolo.
Queste parole stesse sono zattere
prese a nolo sul lago del silenzio
rapide a scomparire nel gran salto.

Sii salda e stammi accanto. Ogni cosa
abbiamo già pagato con la vita.

where sunsets greeted us, happy.
Even these very words are rafts
rented on the lake of silence
quick to vanish in the final leap.

Be steadfast and stand by me.
Everything's been paid for
just by living.

LETTERA MAI SPEDITA

Hai conferito tanto al nostro amore
portandomi trent'anni di domande
corse sotto l'ulivo
mentre il cielo s'apriva rare volte
a fessure di tregua
nel perversante incombere dei corvi.
Molto hai versato
mentre imparavi a vivere
con l'allegria d'una giovane strega
a cui tutto è concesso
anche lavarsi i fianchi col mio latte
e finire di ridere
coprendo il naso col lenzuolo rosso.

LETTER NEVER SENT

Much you've bestowed on our love
bringing me thirty years of questions
under the olive tree
while only rarely did the sky
crack open in signs of truce
amid ever-looming crows.
Much did you tender
while you learned to live
with the cheer of a youthful witch
who can what she wills
even wash her hips with my milk
and laugh to no end
hiding her nose behind the red sheet.

A UN TRADUTTORE

Non è dato sapere come gli astri
abbiano cospirato a trasferire
le mie ossa d'inchiostro fra i tuoi lidi.
Un uomo di rispetto ha asseverato
che era tuo giusto compito
raccogliere il sale che resiste
nel mio verbo, la storia inconsumabile
ordinata per non smutarsi in polvere,
che solo il tuo talento era capace
di preservarne gli echi in altro idioma
giocando lungo il filo dell'enigma.
Allora ci soccorrano
i saldi resti e non ingrate lune
perché prodighe le farfalle del tuo sangue
siano fide compagne nel viaggio
a un canto solitario.

TO A TRANSLATOR

There's no knowing how
the stars conspired
to float my bones of ink to your shores.
A man of some stature maintains
that your proper task
is to sift the salt that resists
in my words, the irreducible story
undestined to dust
whose echoes only your talent
in play along the riddle's edge
could preserve in another tongue.
May, then, the trusty remains
and not ungrateful moons assist us
for the prodigal butterflies of your blood
to be the faithful companions
of a solitary song.

CONTRO I PUGNALI

In cammino, resistendo fra squarci della vita
siamo in pochi ad amarci veramente
i soli che sapranno offrire un fiore
senza attendersi niente.

Quanti versano amore
dentro gli occhi dell'altro?
Rari i porti alle labbra
folto il bosco dei bari.

Ultimi, restiamo qui ostinati
noi che ancora ci amiamo veramente.

Abbracciami abbracciami
lasciami scivolare
sarò una goccia
che scorre fra le pieghe del ventaglio.

AGAINST ALL DAGGERS

In the course of our journey, resisting
amid life's shards, few of us truly learn
to love, the few who'll know how to extend a flower
expecting nothing in return.

How many pour love
in the eyes of the other?
Lips rarely find a harbor,
woods teem with swindlers.

We, the last, resist, obstinately
we who in our love truly persist.

Embrace, embrace me
let me fall
like a drop
slipping in the folds of your fan.

RIPETUTA DOMANDA

A volte ho sospettato di scrivere per me
pratica medicale inflitta a molti.
Giunto al vespro so che così non è
e ho capito di scrivere a me stesso
una ininterrotta epistola nel vuoto
ramaglie nere di un muto delirio.
Perché se guardo bene le mie carte
le intere carte, riconosco sempre
scorci diversi dell'unico viso
forse una sola, ripetuta domanda
come quella del pazzo di paese
figlio e nipote d'un cattivo vino
che va dietro alla banda
e barbuglia nel riso la sua nenia.
Sillabe che non hanno avuto senso
rotolate per terra in poco vento.
E nessun fiore è nato a riscattarle.

A FREQUENT QUESTION

At times I've thought I write for myself
a curative practice inflicted on others.
Now on in years I know otherwise
understand I've been writing to myself
an endless epistle in a vacuum,
charred kindling of a silent raving.
For if I look closely at what I've written—
at all I've written—I always identify
different angles of a selfsame face
perhaps a single, oft-repeated question
like the one mouthed by the village madman
son and grandson of some cheap wine
who struts behind the village band
and drowns his rant in laughter.
Senseless syllables rolling
on the ground in hardly any wind.
Avenged by no flower, ever.

A UN AMICO

Amico, se hai deciso di scordarmi
ti dimenticherò.
Così verrà annientato
il borgo delle difese nostre consuetudini.
Le mie finestre accese sull'attesa
le piazze aperte al ragionare brado
i due cantoni della confidenza
mura fedeli e platani del dono.
Presto
tutto sarà sepolto
nella ferma palude del silenzio
baratro che non lascia trasparire
nessuna traccia.
E, a quanto credo
ti avrò prestato l'ultimo favore.

TO A FRIEND

Friend, if you've opted to forget me,
so will I.
Thus will we demolish
the manor of customs held dear.
My windows in waiting, brightly lit,
the squares of our savage disputes,
the two corners of our confidences,
the trusty walls and benevolent trees.
Soon enough
everything will be buried
in the still marshes of silence,
a chasm that will leave
no trace.
And, in my estimation,
I'll have done you one last favor.

AL LEVAR DEL SIPARIO

ai figli

Lentamente
l'alba perseverava nel suo avvento
ubiquitaria come lume fermo
d'una muta esplosione.
Prima quasi riverbero remoto
d'una saetta restituita al cielo
da terre d'oltremare
poi, algore e fibra
della rivelazione generale
al fine
colata inesorabile di forme
alberi pietre fiori
colpiti al petto
sul fatto di esistere.
Primordi d'un mondo immoto
non mai giunto alla vista
né dunque mai pensato
al levar del sipario
su ognuna
delle storie possibili.

CURTAIN CALL

to my sons and daughters

Slowly
the dawn persevered
in its ubiquitous advent, becalmed light
of a mute explosion.
At first, remote glare
of an arrow returned to the sky
from lands beyond the sea
then, cosmic cold, fiber
of the general revelation
finally
the inexorable flow of forms
trees rocks flowers
heartstruck
at the brink of existence.
Origins of a motionless world
not meant for our eyes
unthought
at the curtain call
of each and every possible
life story.

INEPTIA

Da Omero in poi
sono sempre in cammino
i miei poeti
per tutti i luoghi buoni
a ispirare canzoni
anche se ognuno poi ne cava il suo.
Si vaga
per le terre ed i mari
nel cuore dell'amata
e lungo i cari viali del ricordo
si vaga in solitario
nella storia e nei cieli iperurani
nella pietà e nel fango
comunque a bordo
di eventi vicinissimi e lontani
nel fervere
delle rivoluzioni
tra gli stenti
di pallide emozioni.
Si crede fermamente di vagare
tra i boschi fitti
delle manie proprie
fra pochi chioschi
che dissetano di riparazione
su margini di sintomi e su indizi
di mille iniquità
di veri vizi.

INEPTIA

Ever since Homer
my poets
are always in happy transit
along the byways of the world
inspiring songs
each, ultimately, composing his own.
They wander
over land and sea
by way of the heart of a loved one
and fond paths of memory
they wander alone
through history, across hyperuranic skies
steeped in mud and mercy
straddling events
both near and far
riding the fevers
of revolutions
amid the hardships
of pale emotions.
They wander, obstinately,
through the thick woods
of their own obsessions
amid but a few kiosks
that offer drink and refuge
at the margins of symptoms
and clues of prevailing iniquity,
of genuine vice.

Ma quando
si è bevuto abbastanza
e la gita riesce a perfezione
i miei poeti
riescono a toccare la regione
dove l'anima è stanza.

But when their thirst
is quenched
and the journey comes full circle
my poets all
reach the region
where soul and home are one.

IDENTITA' IN TRANSITO

a Pedro Cano

Grumi indistinti per masse di uno
disfatti in trasparenze
ignote identità dirette contro
fondali densi di colore
corpi in marcia ostinata e solitaria
che affondano nel niente
nella meta d'asfalto ove la vita
continua a squamarsi ogni giorno.
Sono cammini di sostanze inermi
sempre colpite alle spalle
cammini dal passo scaleno
nel meno di forze per altra fatica
di sacchi ed arnesi tenuti per mano
ultimi appigli su cui sostenersi
strenui, come se fossero figli.
Tutti procedono per scomparire
negli abusi di biacca e in assenza di vento.
È ferma solo la forma d'un vecchio
zucchetto rosso al centro della tela
i gomiti sulla transenna che nega l'accesso.
Medita forse il ritorno.

TIANANMEN SQUARE, 20 YEARS LATER

Hell's roots are in the sky,
I once told you. Where the wings
of ravenous crows rattle, creatures
they taught us to call ideas.
Where the fleeting life of freedom
sweeps, soars, glides and disappears
and the vapors of tears drown.
It's in the sky that the voice of prophets
rumbles, inventing the ghosts of gods
and the illusions they loan us to exist.

It was there that the order flashed
to crush with shields of iron
you and two hundred other lilies in bloom
armed to the hilt with only your hearts
steadfast, upright twigs
wearing the red headbands
of martyrdom.

Hell's roots,
remember, are in the sky.
And please, infuse the truth in those to follow.

3-4 June, 2009

PIETAS

Fatti clemente, figlio,
rifiuta l'impostura della forza
prima che ti scudisci la figura
di tuo padre che arranca
piegato e claudicante
verso l'ombra del bosco.

PIETAS

Be merciful, my son,
refuse any and all show of force
before you end up thrashing
your own feeble father
hunched and hobbling
toward the wooded shadows.

DOMINA

Cantare come te
con le mani soltanto,
come te, che dici al vento
ogni bella parola immaginata.

LADY

To sing like you
with hands only,
like you, who utter to the wind
every winsome word imagined.

CONCERNING THE DIFFUSION AND RECREATION OF POETRY: IN PRAISE OF THE LESSER PLAYERS

By Lucio Mariani

Dear friends,

I am well aware of the fact that this brief statement on poetic communication will not be forgiven for deliberately obscuring the figures of poet, publisher, and critic. The latter two, of course, have over the past 150 years, radiantly hegemonized the art's diffusion.

My interest, instead, is to emphasize the role of two minor contributors to the widespread diffusion of the *poiein*: the translator and the public reader. To these figures goes the credit for enabling the poetic work to travel through space and time. Indeed, they deserve to be acknowledged in the way that the history of economics honors the first wayfarer merchants, whose caravans moved artifacts, goods, and food from one land to another, fostering trade and contributing to the spread of knowledge and civilization among different peoples and cultures. Translator and reader, however, deserve more than the merchant of old because, in the practice of a trade no less taxing, they overcome even barriers of time, in anticipation of little or no reward for so obstinately scattering proof of the only art whose existence is questioned in our time.

In all honesty, poetry has never enjoyed much public favor, with the lone exceptions of tragedy and comedy in ancient Greece and republican Rome. Even in the times of the Caesars in Rome, the place of poetry was limited to the higher spheres of the court and senate. Nevertheless, at this moment in time, consideration for both poetry and poet in the Western World has hit an all-time low, on the assumption that neither is useful to our organized societies. Poetic production, in its limited and rarefied offerings, is not much in demand. As a result it has no value, in a world of consumer goods, where time is better spent in the pursuit of every possible material gain. As *New Yorker* editor David Remnick commented in a 2002 interview: "Poetry, unfortunately, is no longer at the center of American or European culture, as it used to be. This is not for any lack of poets, but because it lacks a public." Remnick went on to add a word of hope for those who need none, that is to say for the most celebrated of poets: "And yet there are people reading Montale, Dante, and others, whose ways of thinking and living are deeply changed by the experience."

Poets, translators, and public readers, all players of superfluousness, desperately resist a fate that threatens them with extinction. I suggest that we now direct our attention to their particular forms of resistance, beginning with the figure of translator who, in performing first and foremost an act of devotion (and only secondarily a cultural act), moves poetry from an original linguistic space into other idiomatic spaces. To explain what I mean, please allow me a personal digression.

It is only over the last decade that my own poetry has begun to be translated, and I myself have translated little poetry. I started doing so in 1979, with the exceedingly difficult *"Rondels pour après"*—a section of *Les amours jaunes*, the wonderful collection by Tristan Corbière. I then continued with some poems by the painter Jean-Pierre

Velly, and others by César Vallejo, René Char (from the posthumous *Éloge d'une Soupçonnée*), Yves Bonnefoy, Dana Gioia, and Rosanna Warren. My choice and commitment were animated each and every time by my devotion to texts that I had learned to know and love, in spite of the difficulties and scattered traps of source languages. Even when, in 1991, I was commissioned to translate from Latin into Italian "The Songs of Priapus," I had to acquaint and re-acquaint myself with the text. It was only then that I happily fell in love with the work and gladly accepted the commission.

For to translate poetry is, primarily, an expression of love and respect for the text one confronts: of love insofar as it requires a very difficult process of self-estrangement and identification with the poet, and of respect to the extent that it demands the adoption of a mindset akin to that which characterized the original act of creation. It involves, moreover, a stance that implies the fundamental principles of clarity (as Stendhal used to preach: *"Dans ce genre, on n'émeut que par la clarté"*) and simplicity, which warns us not to sprinkle our rhymes with too much rhetorical salt. To do so, of course, would only deaden their sharpness and value.

On translation, generally, nothing more can be added to the lessons of the past two centuries, though we might do well to recall that it is, in any case, an exercise reserved for "contemplative souls." (There is, however, a recent "contractualist" thesis that cannot go unrecognized, and to which I shall return.) For translation leads us into the most arcane nooks and crannies of linguistic phenomena, because languages are shaped amid differing landscapes and experiences of the world, all of which resonate across different emotional and intellectual registers. The world, in fact, neither is nor appears objectively constituted by "reality," but is differentially segmented and perceived by different peoples and cultures. The world is a continuum of inexhaustible diversity.

By reproducing different modes of observation, languages divide and distinguish us, not because, as languages, they themselves are distinct, but because they are generated by different mental frameworks, by diverse intellectual systems, and, finally, by each language group's own singular conception of life. We not only speak in a given tongue, we think in it as well, moving intellectually through pre-established furrows where our verbal destiny is inscribed. Every language, indeed, assigns to us a specific set of categories and mental maps, which we all deploy in conventional ways. In the words of Borges: "Every language is a tradition, every word a symbol shared; whatever an innovator is capable of altering is irrelevant."

Anyone who wants to translate must possess a rich, colorful, and kaleidoscopic vocabulary in his or her own language, and a better than adequate knowledge of the source language of the poet. He or she will have to be aware of the temptations of the kaleidoscope, and remain committed, again, to the practice of simplicity. He will have to learn to wait, to leave blank spaces on the page, and to make room for silence—all of which are constitutive elements of poetry and the poetic process. It is in this way that the significance of every form of "whitespace" will be respected and given its due.

In this process of transformation, the translator will attempt to reproduce the intentional ambiguities, as well as the mystery, to which the poet has attained within his own linguistic field: this, without burdening the translation with the useless finery, baroque accretions, or ponderous propensities of the target language. Another temptation the good translator will avoid—unless he is perfectly bilingual—is any excessive self-confidence in his or her knowledge of the poet's original tongue.

Where earlier translations are available, he will compare his own solutions with the preceding ones, free of any competitive spirit or prejudice. If rendering the work of a living poet, the translator is well advised to seek him out and get to know him, in as much of a search for aesthetic affinities as for the hidden meanings of his verse. It is through such an attitude that a translator puts himself at the exclusive service of poetry.

In doing so, however, one must never neglect the risks posed by yet another complicating factor: one whose degree of intricacy goes hand-in-hand with the quality of the poem being translated. Let us keep in mind, in fact, that the true mission to which any "greater" poet aspires is for his work to yield and represent a language unto itself: a language that is, unmistakably, one's own. This tension, of course, has nothing to do with the kind of willed experimentation that thrives on gratuitous hermeticisms. Instead, in seeking to expand the limits of metaphor and the horizons of complexity, genuine innovators will enrich the allusive universe of poetics with new forms of "obscurity," wherein semantic and expressive levels will attain to those obscure dimensions which Socrates, for example, admired in Heraclitus (albeit not without a degree of perplexity). And yet, the more successful such attempts—as they overcome the insidiousness of dialogical intertextualism and of what Bakhtin called the "refracted" word—the more the poet's language is forced into a shrinking corner of communicative solitude. (I'm thinking here of the likes of Dickinson, Valéry, Guillén, Mandelstam, Tsvetaeva, Montale, Vallejo, Celan, Char.) And so, he or she will have to wait until speakers of other languages—which include, of course, the translator—will, in time, come to fathom one's own new language, intimately if not consummately.

The way I see things, the same holds for the poet as Ortega y Gasset wrote about the painter (in his *Papeles sobre Velazquez y Goya*): "*Nadie es gran pintor si no es un idioma. Por eso un grande artista no se entiende con nadie*" ("Every great painter is an idiom unto himself. This is why great artists get along with no one"). Nonetheless, it follows that, in a process of linguistic transposition, the price paid by poetry cannot be limited solely to the one exacted by this idiomatic transition. The good translator will have to spend every effort in preserving the emotional impact of the original, in the recreation of a work that will remain substantially faithful to the original text. Diversions—both literal and, on occasion, structural—can thus become necessary and even welcome forms of betrayal, when theoretically mandated by the imperative to maintain the original's precarious balance of sense, sound and representation in the target language. Ultimately a valuable re-creation is reached only in the conception of a translation both "beautiful and unfaithful," as a happy turn of phrase would have it; it is secured, basically, only by reevaluating the Kantian doctrine of taste.

In the old and unresolved dispute between *sourciers* and *ciblistes*, I side with the former. And I also side with George Steiner when he claims, in *After Babel*, that to translate is to relive the poet's original act of creation. (Then again, a like pebble had already been cast into the totalizing pools of structuralism by an Italian, Gianfranco Folena, in a 1973 book titled *Volgarizzare e tradurre*.) And, apropos Steiner, I should add that, nearly thirty years after the publication of *After Babel*, he confirms his judgment in another book of his, *Grammars of Creation*, affirming—with guarded regret—that today's technological mutations are substituting *invention* for *creation*. This, while silence and solitude—the foundations of every creative act—disappear, violated everywhere by the bombardment of the media and by the bombastic frenzy of crowds, who nowadays manage to contaminate even the solemn rites of passage of the deceased.

In sum, attempts to translate poetry will never boil down to mere transpositions and transfers from one language into another.

The translator has to have the capacity to replenish a language's very bloodstream, to perform veritable transplants and grafts which, in saving the life of the patient (namely, the poet's subjective world and cultural humus), can also favor new life in different modes and forms of thought, custom, and culture. As a result, relations of structure and sound will also have to be renewed and reworked so as to facilitate, within another linguistic context, a new audience's direct fruition of what is essentially an applied principle of beauty.

Finally, above and beyond all reasonable interpretive liberties, the translator will be bound to the same principles espoused by Duhamel and Vildrac on the matter of poetic technique: that is to say, *"mais d'abord il faut être un poète."* For at the end of his work, the translator, not unlike the poet, will take stock and assess the results of his efforts, heeding the crude but ever-truthful admonition of G. B. Marino, *"E' del poeta il fin la maraviglia / parlo dell'eccellente e non del goffo / chi non sa far stupir vada alla striglia"* ("Wonder is the poet's aim / of him who excels, and does not stumble / for if one knows not how to amaze, only will he bumble") (*La Murtoleide*, Fischiata XXXIII).

The scope of this paper is such that I have avoided the endless semiotic problems that translation invariably poses. I've done so, on the one hand, out of what I believe to be a healthy sense of my own limitations; on the other hand, these problems have only recently been tackled by an acclaimed and undisputed specialist like Umberto Eco, in an engaging work titled *Experiences in Translation*. In his book, Eco highlights how the work of translation involves a *process of negotiation* among various contending parties: on the one side are the source text, a living author or a deceased author's heirs, and the culture in which the text was born; on the other side stand the translated text, the commissioning publisher, and the target culture with its manifold expectations. Amid these forces and pressures the translator is interposed as a negotiator: this, in short, makes for the "contractualist" thesis to which I earlier referred.

I would now like to spend some words in praise of public readers. The least of caravaneers, even lowlier than translators, they too have great duties and merits. Born in the thinly populated land of poetry lovers (beware, mind you, of actors and professional readers), they pop up here and there, outsiders at the edge of the literary world. Often recruited by the armies of lesser poets, they are disliked by those who—as often happens—don't even know how to read their own poetry. They are unpopular because what they do, they do well, especially in making their talents available only to the poetry they love and choose.

At least in Italy, events and occasions for their readings are rare. For the most part, such chance readings take place in small private circles, generated by what little fame the readers themselves can muster. Like translators, the good readers—in the all-too-few opportunities that Fate affords them—also have and use the ability to transfer poetry into cavities of space and time, toward the elsewhere and the future, where they bring it to people who otherwise would neither have had access to it or sought it out on their own. And as a result, at one and the same time, these readers generate in some people the need for poetry, and in others a certain embarrassment for having, until now, ignored it. Thus it happens that readers, within a void and from out of nowhere, can recreate poetry, by simply presenting it in a dignified manner. These people of good will, who've long discovered and experimented with the interpretative powers of the voice, know that poetry—the art closest to music—is better appreciated and loved the more it is heard. And to this end, what greater vehicle exists than a good performance before an audience with text in hand?

For these reasons, good readers will always be a good poet's best and most generous friends. Like faithful servants, they will rigorously honor the philological echoes and intricacies of any text; moreover, in the humble service of poetry's capacity to generate awe, the reader will, like an inspired oracle, offer that very experience to his or her audience, but with no self-aggrandizement whatsoever. For as Mandelstam once noted: "Reading poetry is a great and most difficult art, and the vocation to read it is no less respectable than the poet's own." These words are excerpted from an essay the poet wrote in 1923, entitled "An Army of Poets," and which may well be worth revisiting. The passage that contains this excerpt, in fact, reads:

> In most cases, those who write poetry are poor and distracted readers. They believe that writing is only suffering. Absolutely unreliable where matters of taste are concerned, uneducated, born non-readers, they are invariably offended by suggestions that they learn how to read before starting out to write. Nor can they imagine in the least that reading poetry is a great and most difficult art, and the vocation to read it is no less respectable than the poet's own. Born non-readers that they are, the humble vocation to read cannot gratify them.

Thus, in closing, I can now reflect back on my opening remarks concerning the twilight of poetry today, and try to identify some of the causes behind this state of affairs. Public education in Italy has, for a long time, done away with the practice of memorizing poems, something now branded as a form of regressive pedagogy and a despicable teaching method. As a result, works by greater and lesser poets alike are only approached through the lens of the critic, who routinely dissects and comments on poems by placing them in theoretical and comparative contexts, where unrelated disciplines like psychology, sociology and history are brought to bear on the analysis.

In this way students do not access the complex emotional pathways that repeated readings and memorization can open up. Thus the Dionysian nerve hidden in each of us doesn't get to surface, let alone be stimulated. And as a result the student doesn't get to make the admittedly difficult but extraordinary experience of knowing a poem directly, on one's own, even if in the silent mnemonic repetitions that are part and parcel of any and all learning, at every stage of life. Instead, the student will be forced to study the soul and signposts of a poem on the basis of commentaries that gloss, dissect, analyze, and, ultimately, shatter the work and end up overshadowing it, while the commentaries themselves become independent objects of study. And let's not forget: even this approach concerns only the few rhymes that have made it, anthologized, into the classroom!

If we think back for a moment on Tzvetan Todorov's "The Abuses of Memory," and his claim that memory derives from the interaction between erasure and preservation, as a procedure that necessitates selective acts, we can see how privileging the critical apparatus over the poetic text can make for an "official version of the poetic past"; that is to say, for a reading of the history of aesthetics that attributes to the teacher (as presumed expert), and robs from the student, "the right to control those elements worthy of preservation." This amounts, in sum, to an operation of aesthetic policing, aimed at promoting cultural sameness and denying the infinite possibilities of individual preference.

It becomes clear, then, how the young intellectual army that is about to intersect and leave its mark on our age (aside from a cluster of maniacs already at work writing more and more critical essays), can only stay away from poetry. These potential priests find it difficult to enter the mindset of getting to know or recognize in poetry a lifetime companion or source of consolation, let alone of aesthetic value. It only follows that, if poetic production has no value, its producer is unworthy of consideration. In other words, he is useless. And what I stated at the outset has, for all sakes and purposes, been proven.

It is good that poets, eccentric men and women with no reason to fear the lotus flower (so little is there of value to remember), should remain confined in their daring solitudes, in their well-stocked menageries, in their monastic cells where, not air and fragrances, but metaphors and ravings flow. This well befits a community of survivors who only inflict pain on their own kind, a race whose extinction would cause no collective anguish. A race so unlike that of the panda, or the hooded seal! In the words of César Vallejo: *"Senõr Ministro de Salud: qué hacer?"* / Ah! *"desgraciadamente, hombres humanos, / hay, hermanos, muchísimo qué hacer"* ("Honorable Secretary of Health, what should we do?" / "Sadly, oh human men / there is, my brothers, so much to do") ("Los nueve monstrous," *Poemas humanos*).

(*Translated by Anthony Molino, in collaboration with Marina Molino*)

Lucio Mariani was born in Rome, where he still makes his home, in 1936. He is the author of twelve books of poetry, including the recent *Canti di Ripa Grande* (Milan: Crocetti, 2013) and the selected poems of *Farfalla e segno: Poesie scelte 1972-2009* (Crocetti, 2010), from which *Traces of Time* is derived. His works have been translated into several languages, including Spanish, French, Greek, and German.

In addition to his own work, Mariani has regularly translated from several languages into Italian. His two primary translations are, from the Latin, *Carmina priapea* (Ponte alle Grazie) and, more recently, a selection of poems by César Vallejo entitled *Il monarca d'ossa* (G. Landolfi). Other poets translated include Corbière, B. M. Koltès, J. P. Velly, Warren, Gioia, and Bonnefoy. An accomplished essayist as well as poet, Mariani has also written for the theatre and published a book of short stories. In 2003, he was awarded Italy's prestigious Cardarelli Prize for poetry.

Anthony Molino is a widely published psychoanalyst, PhD anthropologist, and literary translator. As a translator, he has received a Fulbright scholarship to the University of Florence, three grants from the Pennsylvania Council on the Arts, fellowships from the Academy of American Poets and the National Theater Translation Fund, and an Affiliate Fellowship with the American Academy in Rome. His published translations include, among others, works by Valerio Magrelli, Lucio Mariani, Manlio Santanelli, Eduardo De Filippo, and Antonio Porta, for whose *Kisses, Dreams and Other Infidelities* he received a 2005 Gradiva Award for Poetry. He is presently translating a book of selected poems by Mariangela Gualtieri.

Open Letter—the University of Rochester's nonprofit, literary translation press—is one of only a handful of publishing houses dedicated to increasing access to world literature for English readers. Publishing ten titles in translation each year, Open Letter searches for works that are extraordinary and influential, works that we hope will become the classics of tomorrow.

Making world literature available in English is crucial to opening our cultural borders, and its availability plays a vital role in maintaining a healthy and vibrant book culture. Open Letter strives to cultivate an audience for these works by helping readers discover imaginative, stunning works of fiction and poetry, and by creating a constellation of international writing that is engaging, stimulating, and enduring.

Current and forthcoming titles from Open Letter include works from Argentina, China, France, Greece, Iceland, Israel, Latvia, Poland, South Africa, and many other countries.

www.openletterbooks.org